HF 125 BEN

Library

IRST

D1322968

PRINCE2

This book has been revised in line with the changes to the PRINCE2 manual, published in February/March 2002.

PRINCE2 is a trademark belonging to the Office of Government Commerce and I am indebted to them for their permission to use the name.

PRINCE2
PRACTICAL HANDBOOK
2ND EDITION

COLIN BENTLEY

AMSTERDAM BOSTON HEIDELBERG LONDON NEW YORK OXFORD
PARIS SAN DIEGO SAN FRANCISCO SINGAPORE SYDNEY TOKYO

Butterworth-Heinemann
An imprint of Elsevier
Linacre House, Jordan Hill, Oxford OX2 8DP
200 Wheeler Road, Burlington MA 01803

First published 1997
Reprinted 1998, 1999
Second edition 2002
Reprinted 2002, 2003 (twice)

British Library Cataloguing in Publication Data
A catalogue record for this book is available from the British Library

Library of Congress Cataloguing in Publication Data
A catalogue record for this book is available from the Library of Congress

ISBN 0 7506 53302

For information on all Butterworth-Heinemann publications
visit our website at www.bh.com

Typeset by Keyword Typesetting Services Ltd
Printed and bound in Great Britain by Biddles Ltd,
www.biddles.co.uk

Contents

Computer Weekly Professional Series

There are few professions which require as much continuous updating as that of the IS executive. Not only does the hardware and software scene change relentlessly, but also ideas about the actual management of the IS function are being continuously modified, updated and changed. Thus keeping abreast of what is going on is really a major task.

The Butterworth-Heinemann *Computer Weekly* Professional Series has been created to assist IS executives keep up to date with the management ideas and issues of which they need to be aware.

One of the key objectives of the series is to reduce the time it takes for leading edge management ideas to move from the academic and consulting environments into the hands of the IT practitioner. Thus this series employs appropriate technology to speed up the publishing process. Where appropriate some books are supported by CD-ROM or by additional information or templates located on the Web.

This series provides IT Professionals with an opportunity to build up a bookcase of easily accessible, but detailed information on the important issues that they need to be aware of to successfully perform their jobs as they move into the new millennium.

Aspiring or already established authors are invited to get in touch with me directly if they would like to be published in this series.

Dr Dan Remenyi
Series Editor
Dan.remenyi@mcil.co.uk

1 | **Introduction**

Project management is a very unusual job, but millions of us do it. Project management has been done for centuries. The pyramids, the Great Wall of China, bridges over rivers, holidays, business trips, these are just a few examples of projects.

'Project management is just common sense.' Of course it is. So why do so many of us get it wrong? Even if we get one project right, we probably make a mess of the next. And why do we keep getting it wrong time after time? You need to be armed with a little more than common sense when diving into a project such as constructing a pyramid. It's no good getting half way through, then remembering you forgot to put in the damp course!

Why do so many professionals say they are project managing, when what they are actually doing is fire fighting?

The answer is that, where project management is concerned, most of us don't learn from our mistakes. We don't think about the process, document it, structure it, repeat it and use experience to improve the model. Problems are likely to arise in every project we tackle, but planning ahead and controlling how things happen against that plan could have avoided many of the problems the fire-fighter tackles.

Those who are starting a project for the first time should not have to reinvent the wheel. They should be able to build on the experience of previous Project Managers. By the time we are doing our tenth project we should have a method that helps us avoid mistakes we made in the previous nine.

This book presents the latest version of PRINCE2, a structured project management method based on the experience of scores of other Project Managers who have contributed, some from their mistakes or omissions, others from their success. It can be applied to any kind of project, however big or small, i.e. the basic philosophy is always the same. The method should be tailored to suit the size, importance and environment of the project. Common sense PRINCE2 says, 'Don't use a sledgehammer to crack a walnut', but equally don't agree important things informally where there is any chance of a disagreement later over what was agreed.

Typical Project Problems

So let's have a look at some typical problems from several different points of view.

A few years ago I was asked to implement PRINCE in the computer department of a large international company. They had drawn up a list of six typical complaints from their customers.

- The end product was not what we originally asked for.

- The system and the project changed direction without our realising it.

- The costs escalated without our realising it, then it was too late to stop it.

- We were told the system would be delivered late, but we were only told this when it was too late for us or the computer department to supply extra effort.

- We were in the dark during most of the development, and even now we do not really understand how to make the system work.

- The programs are not reliable, hence maintenance costs are more than we expected.

This was an embarrassing list for them, showing that the customers were ignored during most of the project. This was apart from poor planning and control problems during the project.

Speaking of control, the Hoskyns Group did a survey of projects some years ago and listed symptoms that they found to indicate projects that were out of control. You might recognise some of the symptoms.

- Unclear direction
- Over- or underworked staff
- People and equipment not available when needed
- Examples of rework or wasted effort
- The final tasks were rushed
- Poor quality work
- Projects late and overspent
- Small problems had a big impact.

But why do these problems occur? Their causes show the reasons why a formal project management method is needed.

- Lack of customer involvement
- Lack of coordination
- Lack of communication
- Inadequate planning
- Lack of progress control
- Lack of quality control
- Insufficient measurables.

So there we have it. Without good project management projects will:

- Take more time than expected
- Cost more than expected
- Deliver a product that is not exactly what the customer wants
- Deliver a product of inadequate quality

- Not reveal their exact status until they finish.

These experiences show us why a good project management method such as PRINCE2 is needed if our projects are to be well managed and controlled.

Benefits of a Project Management Method

- The method is repeatable
- The method is teachable
- It builds on experience
- Everyone knows what to expect
- If you take over a project in the middle, you know what documents to look for and where to find them
- There is early warning of problems
- It is proactive not reactive (but has to be prepared to be reactive to events – illness, pregnancy, accident, external event).

Organisations are becoming increasingly aware of the opportunities for adopting a 'project' approach to the way in which they address the creation and delivery of new business products or implement any change. They are also increasingly aware of the benefits that a single, common, structured approach to project management – as is provided through PRINCE2 – can bring.

2	# An Overview of PRINCE2

Key Principles

PRINCE2 is a scalable, flexible project management method, suitable for use on any type of project. It has been derived from professional Project Managers' experiences and refined over years of use in a wide variety of contexts. It is owned by a stable public authority, the Office of Government Commerce (OGC), and is available free of charge in the public domain. The OGC has an ongoing commitment to maintaining the currency of the method, together with the manual and other books used to define the method.

PRINCE2 gives:

- Controlled management of change by the business in terms of its investment and return on investment

- Active involvement of the users of the final product throughout its development to ensure the business product will meet the functional, environmental, service and management requirements of the users

- More efficient control of development resources.

So that is how its users derive the benefits mentioned in the Introduction.

Organisations require a project management method that will meet and fit their particular needs, and PRINCE2 is designed to be flexible and scalable, so it can be 'tailored' to fit and meet these needs.

A key approach of the method is that it firmly distinguishes the **management** of the development process from the **techniques** involved in the development process itself.

There are two key principles of PRINCE2 that you should grasp as the basis for your understanding of the method.

A PROJECT SHOULD BE DRIVEN BY ITS BUSINESS CASE

You shouldn't start a project unless there is a sound Business Case for it. At regular intervals in the project you should check to see that the project is still viable and stop the project if the justification has disappeared.

PRINCE2 IS PRODUCT BASED

PRINCE2 focuses on the **products** to be produced by the project, not the activities to produce them. This affects its method of planning, many of its controls and its approach to ensuring quality.

Structure of the PRINCE2 Method

There are three parts to the structure of the method itself:

- Processes
- Components
- Techniques.

PRINCE2 offers a set of **Processes** that provide a controlled start, controlled progress and a controlled close to any project. The processes explain what should happen, when it should be done and by which role.

PRINCE2 has a number of **Components** to explain its philosophy about various project aspects, why they are needed and how they can be used. This philosophy is implemented through the processes.

PRINCE2 offers only a few **Techniques**. The use of most of them is optional. You may already have a technique that is covering that need satisfactorily. The exception is the product-based planning technique. This is a very important part of the PRINCE2 method. Its understanding and use bring major benefits and every effort should be made to use it.

The table below gives a very high level view of what the processes do and the links between them, the components and the techniques.

COMPONENT	PROCESS	TECHNIQUE
Controls Business Case Organisation Quality Project Approach Risks Controls Planning	**Starting Up a Project (SU)** Establish: • What (in general terms) is the product we're trying to deliver (Project Brief)? • Why it should be done • Are we likely to be better off? • Who is going to pay for it? • Who is going to define what is needed? • Who is going to do the work? • What is the expected quality? • How will we go about providing a solution? • Can we see any risks in doing it? • How the customer and supplier will agree that the project is complete (Acceptance Criteria) • How much effort would it take to draw up a 'contract' (the initiation Stage Plan)?	**Quality Review** **Product-based Planning**

Controls How will the project be controlled? Should the project be divided into pieces for easier planning and control? **Business Case** **Change Control** How will changes to the original request be controlled? **Configuration Management** How will the products be tracked and controlled? **Risk** How risky is the project? **Quality** How will the required quality be built into the products? **Plans** Planning the project	**Initiating a Project (IP)** Draw up a 'contract' which formally states: • What key products the project will deliver • Why there are good reasons for doing the project (Business Case) • The scope of what we are doing • Any constraints which apply to the product we are to deliver • Any constraints applied to the project • Who is to be involved in the project decision making? • How and when the products will be delivered and at what cost (Project Plan) • How we will achieve the required quality (Project Quality Plan) • What risks we face (Risk Log) • How we are going to control the project. Define what the next commitment is for which you are looking (next Stage Plan) Set up a filing structure for the project	**Product-based Planning**

Controls Track progress **Change Control** Capture change requests and analyse their impact **Configuration Management** Keep control of products **Risk** Watch for changes in risk status	**Controlling a Stage (CS)** Allocate work Check on progress Ensure that the quality is OK Ensure that changes are controlled Report on progress Watch for plan deviations Escalate any forecast deviation Update the Stage Plan	**Change Control** Log and analyse the impact of any proposed changes
Plans What should be in my Team Plan? **Controls** Team Manager reports to the Project Manager. Does the Team Manager need to escalate a problem to the Project Manager? **Quality** Are my team producing quality products?	**Managing Product Delivery (MP)** Negotiate work to be done Do it Plan it Keep track of progress Report progress Make a record of quality checks Control changes Give it back	**Quality Review** Is a product free from error? **Change Control** Log any received changes

Plans Preparing the next Stage Plan and updating the Project Plan **Controls** What does the project look like now? **Risk** Has the risk status changed?	**Managing Stage Boundaries (SB)** Gather the results of the current Stage Plan the next part (next Stage Plan) Check the effect on: the Project Plan the justification for the project the risks Report and seek approval	
Controls Has everything been delivered? Is the customer happy? Is everybody happy about the handover of the product? Are there any loose ends?	**Closing a Project (CP)** Check that everything has been delivered Check that the product is accepted Make sure there are no loose ends Plan how and when achievement of the expected benefits can be checked Record any useful information for other projects Report on the success of the project against its Project Initiation Document Store the project records for audit Release resources	

Controls Should we approve the next stage? What do we do about the forecast deviation from the agreed plan?	Directing a Project (DP) Should we approve the next step in the project? Decide on the acceptable margins of plan deviation Confirm project closure	
Plans Structure and explanation of the levels of plan	Planning (PL) A process for the standardised creation of plans	Product-based Planning

PRINCE2 has a process-based approach to project management. The processes define the management activities to be carried out during the project. In addition, PRINCE2 describes a number of components that are applied within the appropriate processes. Figure 2.1 shows the components positioned around the central process model.

The Components

The components of PRINCE2 are:

Business Case   PRINCE2 is based on the premise that a viable Business Case should drive a project. The essential contents are defined and linked with the moments in the processes when the Business Case should be updated or consulted.

Organisation   The structure of a project management team. A definition of the roles, responsibilities and relationships of all staff involved in the project. PRINCE2 describes roles. According to the size and complexity of a project, these roles can be combined or shared.

Plans	PRINCE2 offers a series of plan levels that can be tailored to the size and needs of a project, and an approach to planning based on products rather than activities.
Controls	A set of controls that facilitate the provision of key decision-making information, allowing the organisation to pre-empt problems and make decisions on problem resolution. For senior management PRINCE2 controls are based on the concept of 'management by exception', i.e. if we agree a plan, let the Project Manager get on with it unless something is forecast to go wrong.
Risk	Risk is a major factor to be considered during the life of a project. PRINCE2 defines the key moments when risks should be reviewed, outlines an approach to the analysis and management of risk, and tracks these through all the processes.
Quality	PRINCE2 recognises the importance of quality and incorporates a quality approach to the management and technical processes. It begins by establishing the Customer's Quality Expectations and follows these up by laying down standards and quality inspection methods to be used, and checking that these are being used.
Configuration Management	Tracking the components of a final product and their versions for release is called configuration management. There are many methods of configuration management available. PRINCE2 does not attempt to invent a new one, but defines the essential facilities and information requirements for a configuration management method and how it should link with other PRINCE2 components and techniques.
Change Control	PRINCE2 emphasises the need for change control and this is enforced with a change control technique plus identification of the processes that apply the change control.

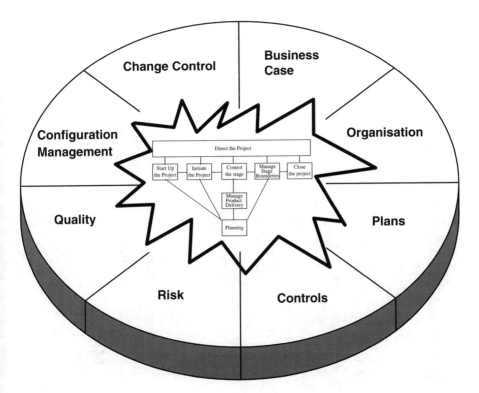

Figure 2.1

The Processes

The steps of project management are described in eight processes, which are summarised in Figure 2.2.

Any project run under PRINCE2 will need to address each of these processes **in some form**. However, the key to successful use of the process model is in tailoring it to the needs of the individual project. Each process should be approached with the question 'How extensively should this process be applied on this project?'

DIRECTING A PROJECT (DP)

This process is aimed at the senior management team responsible for the project, the key decision makers. These are usually very busy people and should be involved in only the decision-making process

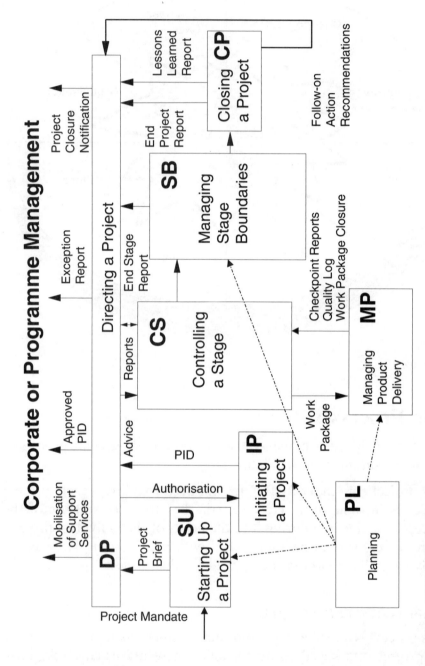

Figure 2.2   PRINCE2 Processes

of a project. PRINCE2 helps them achieve this by adopting the philosophy of 'management by exception'. The DP process covers the steps to be taken by this senior management team (the Project Board) throughout the project from start-up to project closure and has five major steps:

- Authorising the preparation of a Project Plan and Business Case for the project

- Approving the project go-ahead

- Checking that the project remains justifiable at key points in the project life cycle

- Monitoring progress and giving advice as required

- Ensuring that the project comes to a controlled close.

STARTING UP A PROJECT (SU)

This is intended to be a very short pre-project process with five objectives:

- Design and appoint the project management team

- Ensure that the aims of the project are known

- Decide on the approach which will be taken within the project to provide a solution

- Define the Customer's Quality Expectations

- Plan the work needed to draw up the PRINCE2 'contract' between customer and supplier.

INITIATING A PROJECT (IP)

This process prepares the information on whether there is sufficient justification to proceed with the project, establishes a sound management basis for the project and creates a detailed plan for as much of the project as management are in a position to authorise. The management product created is the Project Initiation Document, the baseline against which progress and success will be measured.

CONTROLLING A STAGE (CS)

This process describes the monitoring and control activities of the Project Manager involved in ensuring that a stage stays on course and reacts to unexpected events. The process forms the core of the Project Manager's effort on the project, being the process which handles day-to-day management of the project development activity.

Throughout a stage there will be many cycles of:

- Authorising work to be done
- Gathering progress information about that work
- Watching for changes
- Reviewing the situation
- Reporting
- Noting useful lessons in the Lessons Learned Log
- Taking any necessary action.

The process covers these activities, together with the ongoing work of management of risk and change control.

MANAGING PRODUCT DELIVERY (MP)

This process provides a control mechanism so that the Project Manager and specialist teams can agree details of the work required. This is particularly important where one or more teams are from third party suppliers not using PRINCE2. The work agreed between the Project Manager and the Team Manager, including target dates, quality and reporting requirements, is called a Work Package.

The process covers:

- Making sure that work allocated to the team is authorised and agreed
- Planning the team work
- Ensuring that the work is done

- Ensuring that products meet the agreed quality criteria
- Reporting on progress and quality to the Project Manager
- Obtaining acceptance of the finished products.

MANAGING STAGE BOUNDARIES (SB)

The objectives of this process are to:

- Plan the next stage
- Update the Project Plan
- Update the Business Case
- Update the risk assessment
- Report on the outcome and performance of the stage which has just ended
- Obtain Project Board approval to move into the next stage.

If a major deviation from a Stage Plan is forecast, the Project Board may request the Project Manager to produce an Exception Plan (see Chapter 14 for an explanation), this process also covers the steps needed for that.

CLOSING A PROJECT (CP)

The process covers the Project Manager's work to request the Project Board's permission to close the project either at its natural end or at a premature close decided by the Project Board. The objectives are to:

- Note the extent to which the objectives set out at the start of the project have been met
- Confirm the customer's satisfaction with the products
- Confirm that maintenance and support arrangements are in place (where appropriate)
- Make any recommendations for follow-on actions

- Ensure that all lessons learned during the project are annotated for the benefit of future projects

- Report on whether the project management activity itself has been a success or not

- Prepare a plan to check on achievement of the product's claimed benefits.

PLANNING (PL)

Planning is a repeatable process, used by several of the other processes whenever a plan is required. The process makes use of the PRINCE2 product-based planning technique and covers:

- Designing the plan

- Defining and analysing the plan's products

- Identifying the necessary activities and dependencies

- Estimating the effort required

- Scheduling resources

- Analysing the risks

- Adding text to describe the plan, its assumptions and the quality steps.

Structure of this Book

Having gone through an introduction and overview of the method, the book will focus on the processes as the main theme. This will provide a project skeleton and a general project timeframe. Where appropriate there will be links to the components and to examples of forms that could be used in the processes. The book also includes sample descriptions of the PRINCE2 roles.

3 | Starting Up a Project (SU)

Top Level Diagram

See Figure 3.1.

WHAT DOES THE PROCESS DO?

- Appoints the project management team

- Completes (or confirms the existence of) terms of reference for the project

- Identifies the type of solution to be provided (the Project Approach)

- Identifies the Customer's Quality Expectations

- Creates a Risk Log and enters into it any risks known already or discovered in the work of this process

- Plans the initiation stage.

WHY?

To establish:

- What is to be done

- Who will make the decisions

- Who is funding the project

- Who will say what is needed

- What quality standards are required

INPUT   **OUTPUT**

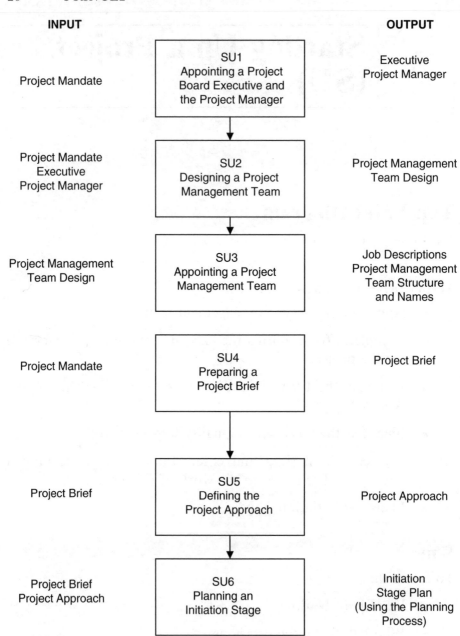

Project Mandate	SU1 Appointing a Project Board Executive and the Project Manager	Executive Project Manager
Project Mandate Executive Project Manager	SU2 Designing a Project Management Team	Project Management Team Design
Project Management Team Design	SU3 Appointing a Project Management Team	Job Descriptions Project Management Team Structure and Names
Project Mandate	SU4 Preparing a Project Brief	Project Brief
Project Brief	SU5 Defining the Project Approach	Project Approach
Project Brief Project Approach	SU6 Planning an Initiation Stage	Initiation Stage Plan (Using the Planning Process)

Figure 3.1

- Who will provide the resources to do the work.

How?

See Figure 3.2.

SU1 – Appointing a Project Board Executive and Project Manager

WHAT DOES THE PROCESS DO?

- Appoints the Executive and Project Manager, prepares and signs job descriptions.

WHY?

Every project needs a sponsor, the key decision maker, the provider of funds. But normally this person is too busy to manage the project on a day-to-day basis. So we also need a Project Manager to do the planning and control. We need to identify these two people before anything can happen (in a controlled manner) in a project.

RESPONSIBILITY

Corporate or programme management should appoint these two roles.

How?   LINKS TO OTHER PARTS OF THE BOOK

- Corporate or programme management   Organisation
  identify the Executive to be responsible for
  the project
- Either corporate/programme management or
  the Executive or both identify a suitable
  Project Manager

- The standard PRINCE2 role descriptions are tailored by discussion between senior management, the Executive and Project Manager | Team Roles

- The tailored roles are typed up, both people sign two copies of their job descriptions. The individual keeps one, the other is kept by the Project Manager for filing once the project filing system has been set up.

IN PRACTICE

The Executive should have strong links with the senior management group responsible for this appointment. Ideally for major projects the Executive should be one of that senior management group, e.g. a member of the programme management team. It is necessary to have a strong bond of confidence between corporate/programme management and the Executive. This person will be making key decisions on their behalf. If the higher level of management wants to check every decision made by the Executive, this will slow down the whole project process. The relationship between the Executive and corporate/programme management should be similar to that between the Project Board and the Project Manager, i.e. 'As long as work is progressing within laid down constraints, then get on with it. We will back you up.'

FOR SMALL PROJECTS

A small project is more likely to be stand-alone. There may be no corporate or programme management involved with the project. In this case the sponsor becomes the Executive by default and would appoint the Project Manager personally.

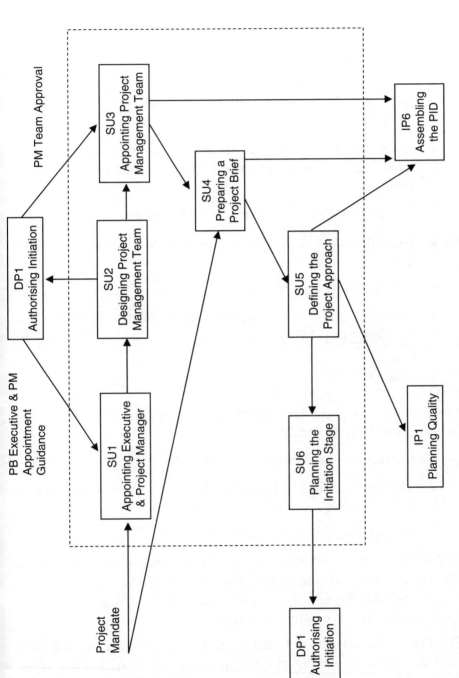

Figure 3.2

SU2 – Designing a Project Management Team

WHAT DOES THE PROCESS DO?

- Proposes the other Project Board members (unless these have already been selected by corporate/programme management)

- Discusses with the Project Board members whether they will need help to carry out their Project Assurance responsibilities

- Design any Project Assurance roles that are to be delegated

- Identifies candidates for any delegated Project Assurance roles

- Identifies any required Team Managers

- Identifies any Project Support requirements, particularly a Configuration Librarian.

WHY?

The complete project management team needs to reflect the interests, and have the approval of:

- Corporate/programme management

- The users of the final product, those who will specify details of the required product

- The supplier(s) of that product.

Project Board members must decide whether they want independent checks on their particular interests in the project as the project progresses (the Project Assurance part of the role), or whether they can do this verification themselves.

The Project Manager has to decide if any administrative support is needed, such as planning and control tool expertise, configuration management, filing or help with specialist techniques.

RESPONSIBILITY

The Executive is responsible for the work of the process, but is likely to delegate much of the work to the Project Manager.

HOW?	LINKS TO OTHER PARTS OF THE BOOK
• Identify customer areas that will use or control the end product, the commitment required and the level of authority and decision making which is suitable for the criticality and size of the project (Senior User)	Organisation
• Identify who will provide the end product(s) (Senior Supplier) and the level of commitment and authority required from them	
• Identify candidates for the roles	
• Check out their availability and provisional agreement	
• Check whether the Project Board members will carry out their own Project Assurance responsibility	Organisation
• Try to find out what volume of change requests might come in during the project. If it is high, discuss with the proposed Project Board if they want to appoint a Change Authority to handle change request decisions.	Change Control
• Identify candidates for any Project Assurance functions which are to be delegated	Roles
• Check out their availability	
• Decide if any Project Support will be required	Roles
• Identify resources for any required support.	

IN PRACTICE

Corporate/programme management may have already defined some or all of the composition of the Project Board, particularly where the project is part of a programme.

If the project is part of a programme, the use of the programme's assurance and support functions may be imposed.

If the management of many different user areas is looking for Project Board representation, it may be more effective to form a user committee, whose chairperson represents all their interests on the Project Board.

In theory the Project Board should decide on what action to take about Project Issues. If the volume of submitted changes is likely to be high, the board may choose to appoint a change authority to assess all Project Issues on their behalf. This change authority might, for example, be the same body as those charged with Project Assurance, or may be a small group of representative user managers. If appointed, the Project Board should give a change budget to such a body. This is usually accompanied by a couple of constraints, such as 'No more than X on any one change, no more than Y spent in any stage without reference to the Project Board.'

FOR SMALL PROJECTS

It would be normal for Project Board members to carry out their own Project Assurance. In very small projects the Executive and Senior User roles will often be combined. If a department is developing a product for its own use and all the project's resources are from that department, the Senior Supplier and Senior User may also be the same person as the Executive.

SU3 – Appointing a Project Management Team

WHAT DOES THE PROCESS DO?

- The other Project Board members, any required Project Assurance and Project Support roles are appointed. There may also be Team Managers to be appointed, particularly for the early stages.

WHY?

A job description for each member of the project management team needs to be agreed with the individual.

After the project management team has been designed, the appointments need to be confirmed by corporate/programme management.

RESPONSIBILITY

Executive, assisted by the Project Manager.

HOW?

	LINKS TO OTHER PARTS OF THE BOOK
• The project management team design is presented to corporate/programme management for approval	
• The Executive informs each project management team member of their appointment	
• The Project Manager discusses and agrees each member's job description with them.	Team Roles

IN PRACTICE

Each project management team member signs two copies of the agreed job description. The person concerned retains one copy, the other copy is filed in the project files. This ensures that there is no later disagreement on who is responsible for what.

FOR SMALL PROJECTS

There may be no need to get approval from any higher level of authority than the Executive. There may be no Project Support functions. If Project Board roles are to be amalgamated, it may be sufficient to use the standard role descriptions listed in this book.

SU4 – Preparing a Project Brief

WHAT DOES THE PROCESS DO?

- Fills in any gaps in the Project Mandate that was handed down.

WHY?

To ensure that sufficient information is available for the Project Board to decide if it wishes to proceed into initiation.

RESPONSIBILITY

The Project Manager is responsible for examining the Project Mandate and collecting any missing details.

HOW?	LINKS TO OTHER PARTS OF THE BOOK
• Compare the information available about the required project against the information required by the Project Board in order to approve project initiation	Project Brief Product Description
• Advise the Project Board how long it will take to prepare for the meeting to authorise the initiation stage	DP1

- Gather any missing information
- Create the Risk Log for the project and add to it any risks shown up in the Project Brief   Forms
- Check the Business Case with the Executive.   Business Case Product Description

IN PRACTICE

Project Mandate is a general term to describe the trigger for the project. The Project Mandate handed down to the Project Manager may be a full specification of the problem, a brief, written request to 'look into' something or 'do something about...', or even a verbal request. The tasks of the process SU4 will be to turn this request (over whose format there may have been no control by the Project Manager) into a Project Brief, a complete set of terms of reference.

If the project is part of a programme, a Project Brief may have already been provided, thus rendering this process unnecessary.

The Project Manager should remember that it is a responsibility of the Project Board, particularly the Executive, to produce the Business Case, not the Project Manager.

The Project Manager should informally check out the Project Brief with Project Board members to ensure there are no problems before formal presentation.

FOR SMALL PROJECTS

There may be pressure on the Project Manager to 'get on with the job' and start with incomplete terms of reference. This should be resisted as it opens up the possibility of disagreement later on what the project was supposed to do (scope). The Project Manager also needs to know how much the solution is worth in order to make appropriate judgements if changes occur later.

SU5 – Defining Project Approach

WHAT DOES THE PROCESS DO?

- Decides on what kind of a solution (Project Approach) will be provided and the general method of providing that solution
- Identifies the skills required by the Project Approach
- Identifies any timing implications of the Project Approach.

The main Project Approaches to be considered are:

- Build a solution from scratch
- Take an existing product and modify it
- Give the job to another organisation to do for you
- Buy a ready-made solution off the shelf.

WHY?

The Project Approach will affect the timescale and costs of the project, plus possibly its scope and quality. This information should be made available to the Project Board in deciding whether to initiate the project.

A check should be made that the proposed Project Approach is in line with the customer's (or programme) strategy.

RESPONSIBILITY

The Project Manager is responsible for the process, assisted by any appropriate Project Support and specialist skills.

HOW?	LINKS TO OTHER PARTS OF THE BOOK
Identify any time, money, resource, support or extension constraints	
• Check for any direction or guidance on Project Approach from earlier documents such as the Project Mandate	Project Mandate Product Description
• Identify any security constraints	
• Check for any corporate/programme statement of direction which might constrain the choice of Project Approach	
• Consider how the product might be brought into use and whether there are any problems which would impact the choice of Project Approach	
• Produce a range of alternative Project Approaches	
• Identify the training needs of the alternatives	
• Compare the alternatives against the gathered information and constraints	
• Prepare a recommendation.	Project Approach Product Description

IN PRACTICE

The customer needs to think very carefully about the Project Approach. Preparation of the above information can avoid the customer being pushed into a Project Approach which is favoured by a supplier, but which turns out to have later problems for the customer, such as lack of flexibility or maintenance difficulties.

FOR SMALL PROJECTS

The question is equally valid for small projects. The pressure to start work on a solution may lead to pressure not to perform this process, but this should be resisted.

SU6 – Planning an Initiation Stage

WHAT DOES THE PROCESS DO?

• Produces a plan for the initiation stage of the project.

WHY?

Preparing a document to get approval to start the project is important work. It needs planning, and since initiation will consume some resources, the Project Board should approve the plan for it.

RESPONSIBILITY

The Project Manager.

HOW?	LINKS TO OTHER PARTS OF THE BOOK
• Examine the Project Brief and decide how much work is needed in order to produce the Project Initiation Document	PID Product Description
• Evaluate the time needed to create the Project Plan	Planning (PL)
• Evaluate the time needed to create the next Stage Plan	
• Evaluate the time needed to create or refine the Business Case	
• Evaluate the time needed to perform risk analysis	Risk

- Create a plan for the initiation stage
- Get Project Board approval for the plan.

Planning (PL)

DP1

IN PRACTICE

The initiation stage should be short and inexpensive compared to the cost and time of the whole project, say 2 or 3 per cent of the whole.

The Project Initiation Document is an extension of the Project Brief to include details of the project management team and risk analysis, plus a refinement of the Business Case and the Project Plan. The initiation Stage Plan should show the effort and resources to generate the extra information and the plan for the next stage.

If informal communication with members of the Project Board is to be frequent during initiation, this can reduce the need for formal reporting.

FOR SMALL PROJECTS

Initiation may only take a matter of an hour or two and therefore may not need a formal plan.

4 | Initiating a Project (IP)

Top Level Diagram

See Figure 4.1.

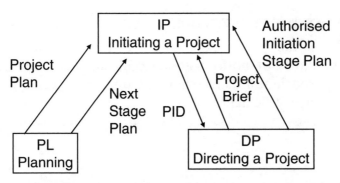

Figure 4.1

WHAT DOES THE PROCESS DO?

- Defines the quality responsibility and quality methods and tools to be used

- Plans the whole project

- Lays the foundation for a well-planned and controlled project

- Confirms the existence of a viable Business Case

- Reassesses the risks facing the project

- Gets all the decision makers signed up to the project.

WHY?

All stakeholders with interest in the project should reach agreement before major expenditure starts on what is to be done and why it is being done.

HOW?

See Figure 4.2.

IP1 – Planning Quality

WHAT DOES THE PROCESS DO?

- Takes the quality expectations of the customer, the quality standards of both customer and supplier and the Project Approach and defines how the quality expected by the customer will be achieved.

WHY?

To be successful, the project must deliver a quality product, as well as meeting time and cost constraints. The means of achieving quality must be specified before work begins.

Quality work cannot be planned until the Customer's Quality Expectations are known.

The time and cost of the project will be affected by the amount of quality work that has to be done, therefore quality planning must be done before a realistic Project Plan can be produced.

RESPONSIBILITY

The Project Manager and those with Project Assurance responsibilities are responsible for quality planning.

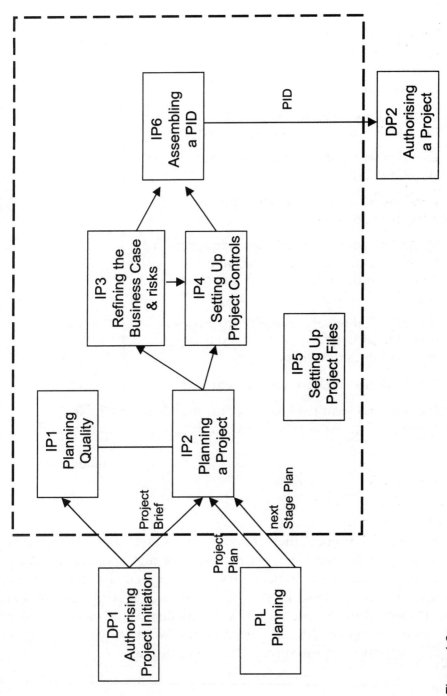

Figure 4.2

How?	Links to Other Parts of the Book
• Establish the Customer's Quality Expectations	Quality (P 144)
• Establish links to any corporate or programme quality assurance function	
• Establish what the customer's quality standards are	
• Establish what the supplier's quality standards are	
• Decide if there is a need for an independent quality assurance function to have representation on the project management team	
• Identify quality responsibility for project products of both the customer and supplier in their job descriptions	Team Roles
• Establish how quality will be achieved	
• Identify any required change control and configuration management procedures.	Change control and configuration management

In practice

For in-house projects there may be no doubt about the quality standards to be used, but where customer and supplier are from different companies it is necessary to agree and document which standards will be used. In such circumstances it is important that the Project Manager specifies how the quality of the products from the supplier will be checked. Sensibly, this would be done by customer involvement in the supplier's quality testing.

FOR SMALL PROJECTS

Even if the customer leaves the quality checking to the developer, there should be customer involvement in specifying the testing environment and the test situations with which the products should successfully cope.

IP2 – Planning Project

WHAT DOES THE PROCESS DO?

- Produces the Project Plan

- Invokes the process SB1 (plan the next stage) to produce the next Stage Plan.

WHY?

As part of its decision on whether to proceed with the project, the Project Board needs to know how much it will cost and how long it will take. Details of the Project Plan also feed into the Business Case to indicate the viability of the project.

If the Project Board makes a general decision to proceed with the project, it needs to have more detailed information about the costs and time of the next stage before committing the required resources.

RESPONSIBILITY

The Project Manager is responsible for the products of the process. There may be help from any Project Support appointed, and drafts of the plan should be checked with those carrying out Project Assurance functions, particularly in terms of the quality work.

How?	Links to other parts of the book
• Use the 'Planning' process to create the Project Plan	Planning (PL)
• Review any project constraints	
• Analyse project risks	
• Modify the plan accordingly	
• Decide on a suitable breakdown of the project into stages	Stages
• Produce the next Stage Plan	SB1
• Check that both plans meet the requirements of the Project Quality Plan	IP1
• Check the plans informally with the Project Board.	

In practice

A Project Plan is always needed. The breakdown into stages may be encouraged by considerations other than just the project size. Examples might be risk assessment, major cash flow moments (invoice payment, invoice submission), and Project Board membership changes.

For small projects

It may not be necessary to produce physically separate Stage Plans if the Project Plan can hold sufficient detail to allow day-to-day control. The Project Manager should decide at what point the inclusion of sufficient detail makes the plan too large to grasp in totality.

IP3 – Refining the Business Case and Risks

WHAT DOES THE PROCESS DO?

- Takes whatever outline Business Case exists for the project, plus the Project Plan, and creates a full Business Case for inclusion in the Project Initiation Document

- Carries out risk analysis for the project.

WHY?

Before commitment to the project it is important to ensure that there is sufficient justification for the resource expenditure. It is also important to have checked that the risks involved in doing the project are acceptable or that plans have been made to avoid, reduce or contain the risks.

RESPONSIBILITY

The responsibility for the Business Case rests with the Executive, probably with input of reasons from the user(s).

HOW?	LINKS TO OTHER PARTS OF THE BOOK
• If an outline Business Case was included in the Project Mandate, check if its circumstances and assumptions have changed	Business Case
• Investigate the work reasons for the project with the customer	
• Investigate the business reasons for the project with the Executive	
• Quantify the benefits wherever possible	Business Case
• Incorporate the costs from the Project Plan	
• Perform risk analysis	Risk

- Modify the Project Plan to reflect any changes caused by risk analysis.

IN PRACTICE

The Project Manager will normally have the work of pulling together the various inputs to the Business Case and performing risk analysis.

If the project is part of a programme, the programme will provide the overall Business Case. In such cases it may be sufficient in the Project Initiation Document to point to the programme's Business Case.

FOR SMALL PROJECTS

It is easy to start small projects without confirming that there are good business reasons for doing it. It is important, however small the project, to go through the exercise of justification. Otherwise, late in the budget year, it may be found that several unjustified projects have consumed the budget now needed for an important larger project.

IP4 – Setting Up Project Controls

WHAT DOES THE PROCESS DO?

- Establishes control points and reporting arrangements for the project, based on the project's size, criticality, risk situation, the customer's and supplier's control standards, and the diversity of interested parties.

WHY?

In order to keep the project under control it is important to ensure that:

- The right decisions are made by the right people at the right time

- The right information is given to the right people at the right frequency and timing.

RESPONSIBILITY

The Project Manager is responsible for establishing the monitoring and reporting necessary for day-to-day control, and agreeing the correct level of reporting and decision points for the Project Board to ensure management by exception.

How?	LINKS TO OTHER PARTS OF THE BOOK
• Agree the stage breakdown with the Project Board	Project Controls
• Agree the format of reports to the Project Board	Highlight Report
• Agree the frequency of Project Board reports	Project Controls
• Establish the frequency of Stage Plan updates	
• Create a Communication Plan covering required input and output information during the life of the project	
• Check that there are sufficient risk and Business Case monitoring activities in the plans	Risk
• Set up a blank Lessons Learned Log to record useful points throughout the project.	Lessons Learned Log

IN PRACTICE

If there are comprehensive control standards in existence it may be sufficient to point to the manual containing them, mention any which will not apply or detail any extra ones. The frequency of reports and controls should still be agreed for the project.

FOR SMALL PROJECTS

It may be acceptable to the Project Board that many of the reports are given verbally. But there should always be a formal initiation and a formal close.

IP5 – Setting Up Project Files

WHAT DOES THE PROCESS DO?

- Sets up the filing structure for management and quality records for the project. Filing or storage needs for the specialist products will depend on the type of products being produced.

WHY?

It is important to retain details of key events, decisions and agreements. These details may help in future project estimation, provide input to the Lessons Learned Log or provide a historical record of what happened, when and why. This is particularly important if relationships between customer and supplier turn sour because of, for example, disputes on scope or costs.

RESPONSIBILITY

The Project Manager is responsible. Project Support may do the work if such resources have been made available.

HOW?	LINKS TO OTHER PARTS OF THE BOOK
• Create the Issue Log	Change Control
• Create the Quality Log	Quality
• Create project and stage files	Configuration Management

• Decide on any configuration management method requirements.	Configuration Management; Project Quality Plan

IN PRACTICE

By this time consideration must be given to any need for configuration management, particularly for the specialist products. There may be a standard method used by either the customer or supplier that is mandated for the project's products. If the project is part of a programme, the configuration management method used should be the same as that of the programme.

The main question about configuration management is the need for it throughout the product's operational life.

FOR SMALL PROJECTS

A full-blown configuration management method may not be required, but consideration should be given to some kind of version control.

IP6 – Assemble the Project Initiation Document

WHAT DOES THE PROCESS DO?

- • Gathers together the information from the other IP processes, assembles the Project Initiation Document and the next Stage Plan.

WHY?

The Project Initiation Document encapsulates all the information needed for the Project Board to make the decision on whether to go ahead with the project or not. It also forms a formal record of the information on which the decision was based, and can be used after the project finishes to judge how successful the project was.

RESPONSIBILITY

The Project Manager is responsible for the assembly with the help of any appointed Project Support and the advice of those with Project Assurance responsibility.

HOW?

- Assemble the required information

- Decide how best to present the information
- Create the Project Initiation Document
- Distribute it to the Project Board, any others with Project Assurance roles, and any others as directed by the Project Board.

LINKS TO OTHER PARTS OF THE BOOK

PID Product Description

IN PRACTICE

Discuss with the Project Board whether it wants the Project Initiation Document to present all the information in full, or whether certain sections, such as Product Descriptions and job descriptions, can be referred to but not included.

FOR SMALL PROJECTS

The Project Initiation Document should be a small document. The Product Description appendix (Appendix 1) describes a Project Initiation Document summary that can be used for small projects (and larger ones, too).

5 | Directing a Project (DP)

Top Level Diagram

See Figure 5.1.

WHAT DOES THE PROCESS DO?

- Authorises project initiation
- Provides liaison with corporate/programme management
- Advises the Project Manager of any external business events which might impact the project
- Approves Stage Plans
- Approves stage closure
- Decides on any changes to approved products
- Approves any Exception Plans
- Gives ad hoc advice and direction throughout the project
- Safeguards the interests of the customer and supplier
- Approves project closure.

WHY?

Day-to-day management is left to the Project Manager, but the Project Board must exercise overall control and take the key decisions.

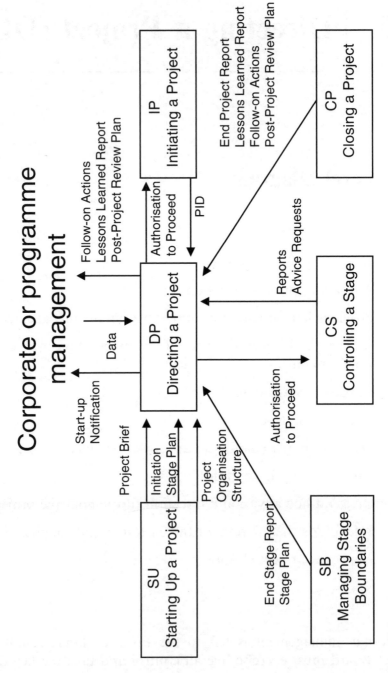

Figure 5.1

How?

See Figure 5.2.

DP1 – Authorising Initiation

WHAT DOES THE PROCESS DO?

- Checks that adequate terms of reference exist
- Checks and approves the initiation Stage Plan
- Commits the resources required to carry out the initiation stage work.

WHY?

The initiation stage confirms that a viable project exists and that everybody concerned agrees what is to be done. Like all project work, the effort to do this needs the approval of the Project Board.

RESPONSIBILITY

The Project Board is responsible, based on information provided by the Project Manager and those with Project Assurance responsibility.

How?

LINKS TO OTHER PARTS OF THE BOOK

How?	Links to other parts of the book
• Confirm the terms of reference, checking if necessary with corporate/programme management	Project Brief Product Description
• Check the initiation Stage Plan and approve it if satisfied	
• Agree tolerance margins for the initiation stage	Project Controls

Corporate or Programme Management

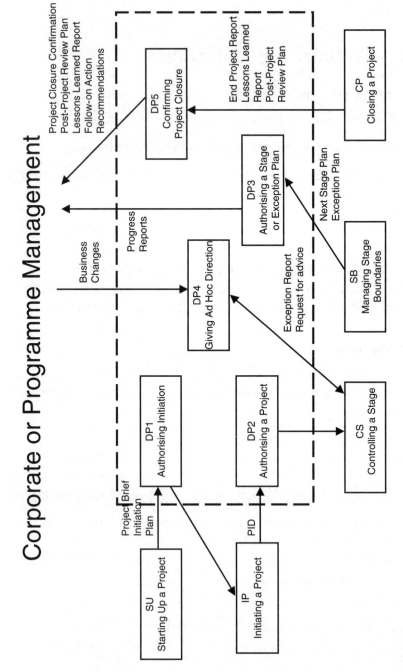

Figure 5.2

- Agree control and reporting arrangements for the initiation stage

- Commit the resources required by the next Stage Plan.

IN PRACTICE

The Project Board should expect to be heavily involved in the initiation stage's work, and therefore should check on and advise the Project Manager of its own availability during the stage.

FOR SMALL PROJECTS

This can be done informally if the Project Board feels that that is suitable. The stage may be so short that no reporting during the stage is required.

DP2 – Authorising a Project

WHAT DOES THE PROCESS DO?

- Decides whether to proceed with the project or not

- Approves the next Stage Plan.

WHY?

The process allows the Project Board to check before major resource commitment that:

- A reasonable Business Case for the project exists

- The project's objectives are in line with corporate or programme strategies and objectives

- The project's estimated duration and cost are within acceptable limits

- The risks facing the project are acceptable

- Adequate controls are in place.

RESPONSIBILITY

The Project Board with advice from those with Project Assurance responsibility.

HOW?	LINKS TO OTHER PARTS OF THE BOOK
• Confirm that the project's objectives and scope are clearly defined and understood by all	Project Brief
• Confirm that the objectives are in line with corporate/programme objectives	
• Confirm that all authorities and responsibilities are agreed	Team Roles
• Confirm that the Business Case is adequate, clear and, wherever possible, measurable	Business Case Product Description
• Confirm the existence of a credible Project Plan that is within the project constraints	Plans
• Check that the plan for the next stage is reasonable and matches that portion of the Project Plan	
• Have any desired changes made to the draft Project Initiation Document	
• Confirm deviation limits for the project and the next stage	Project Controls
• Give written approval for the next stage (or not, if unhappy with any of the details)	
• Arrange a date for the next stage's end stage assessment.	Project Controls

IN PRACTICE

The Project Manager should have been in regular informal contact with the Project Board to ensure that there will be no surprises when the Project Initiation Document is presented. If this contact has been maintained, the above list should be a quick confirmation.

If some minor item in the Project Initiation Document needs further work, but in general the Project Board is happy, approval to proceed can be given with the proviso that the corrective work be done – usually with a target date.

Very often the Project Board members are so busy with day-to-day duties that it is not easy to arrange an end stage assessment at short notice. It is better to plan the next end stage assessment date at the end of the previous stage.

FOR SMALL PROJECTS

The Project Initiation Document details may have been discussed and agreed to informally over a (short) period of time. It may be sufficient for the Project Board to give the go-ahead when the last piece of information is presented without a formal full presentation. Approval to proceed should still be confirmed in writing as an important management document.

DP3 – Authorising a Stage or Exception Plan

WHAT DOES THE PROCESS DO?

- The process authorises each stage (except initiation) and any Exception Plans that are needed.

WHY?

An important control for the Project Board is to approve only one stage at a time. At the end of one stage the Project Manager has to justify both progress so far and the plan for the next stage before being allowed to continue.

RESPONSIBILITY

The Project Board carries responsibility for this process, based on information provided by the Project Manager and with advice from any separate Project Assurance responsibility.

How?	LINKS TO OTHER PARTS OF THE BOOK
• Compare the results of the current stage against the approved Stage Plan	
• Assess progress against the Project Plan	
• Assess the acceptability of the next Stage Plan against the Project Plan	
• Review the prospects of achieving the Business Case	
• Review the risks facing the project	Risk
• Get direction from corporate/programme management if the project is forecast to exceed tolerances or there is a change to the Business Case	Project Controls
• Review tolerances and reporting arrangements for the next stage	Project Controls
• Give approval to move into the next stage (if satisfied).	

IN PRACTICE

The Project Board can stop the project for any reason, e.g. if the Business Case becomes invalid, project tolerances are going to be exceeded, product quality is unacceptable, or the risks become unacceptably high.

If the end stage assessment date was arranged some time ago and occurs before the actual end of the stage, the Project Board can give provisional approval to proceed based on one or more target dates being met to complete the current stage.

If the stage finishes before the planned assessment date, interim approval can be given to do some of the next stage work before formal approval is given. In such a case, the Project Board would clarify what work was to be done before the assessment, rather than give carte blanche to the Project Manager.

FOR SMALL PROJECTS

The decisions can be made informally, but the Project Board should still carry out the above activities and a record be kept of the decisions.

DP4 – Giving Ad Hoc Direction

WHAT DOES THE PROCESS DO?

- Advises the Project Manager about any external events which impact the project

- Gives direction to the Project Manager when asked for advice or a decision about a Project Issue

- Advises on or approves any changes to the project management team

- Makes decisions on the actions to take on receipt of any Exception Reports.

WHY?

There may be a need for occasional Project Board direction outside end stage assessments.

RESPONSIBILITY

The Project Board.

How?	Links to Other parts of the book
• Check for external events, such as business changes, which might affect the project's Business Case or risk exposure	
• Monitor any allocated risk situations	
• Make decisions on any Exception Reports	Project Controls
• Ensure that the project remains focused on its objectives and achievement of its Business Case	
• Keep corporate/programme management advised of project progress	
• Make decisions about any necessary changes to the project management team	Organisation
• Make decisions on Project Issues brought to the attention of the Project Board.	Change Control

In practice

The key activity in this process is deciding what action should be taken on Project Issues, including requests for change and off-specifications. The procedure to be followed should have been agreed and documented in the Project Initiation Document.

This process does not encourage general interference with the work of the Project Manager. The need for Project Board direction will be triggered by either a problem reported in a Highlight Report or an Exception Report, or an external event that it is monitoring on behalf of the project.

For small projects

It may be sufficient for the Project Board and Project Manager to agree informally how to action a Project Issue as soon as it is documented.

DP5 – Confirming Project Closure

WHAT DOES THE PROCESS DO?

- Checks that the objectives of the project have been met

- Checks that there are no loose ends

- Advises senior management of the project's termination

- Recommends a plan for checking on achievement of the expected benefits.

WHY?

There must be a defined end point in a project in order to judge its success. The Project Board must assure itself that the project's products have been handed over and are acceptable. Where contracts (and money) are involved, there must be agreement between customer and supplier that the work contracted has been completed.

RESPONSIBILITY

The Project Board is responsible, advised by the Project Manager and any Project Assurance responsibility.

HOW?

LINKS TO OTHER PARTS OF THE BOOK

- The supplier gains acceptance from the customer that all the required products have been delivered and the acceptance criteria have been met

  Project Controls

- Check that there has been a satisfactory handover of the finished product(s) to those responsible for its use and support

- Check that there are no outstanding Project Issues

  Change Control

• Approve the Follow-on Action Recommendations and pass them to the appropriate group	Product Description
• Approve the Lessons Learned Report and pass it to the appropriate body	Product Description
• Approve the End Project Report	Product Description
• Release the resources allocated to the project	
• Advise corporate/programme management of the project's closure	
• The Project Board disbands the project management team.	

IN PRACTICE

It is sensible for the Project Manager to obtain written confirmation from the users and those who will support the final product that they have accepted the outcome of the project.

FOR SMALL PROJECTS

Not all the reports may be needed, but there should still be a formal sign-off by the Project Board to close the project.

6 | Controlling a Stage (CS)

Top Level Diagram

See Figure 6.1.

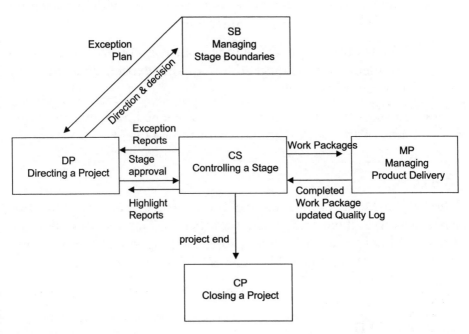

Figure 6.1

WHAT DOES THE PROCESS DO?

- Manages the stage from stage approval to completion.

WHY?

The production of the stage's products within budget and schedule and to the required quality must be driven by the Project Manager and also requires careful monitoring and control.

HOW?

See Figure 6.2.

CS1 – Authorising Work Package

WHAT DOES THE PROCESS DO?

- Allocates work to be done to a team or individual, based on the needs of the current Stage Plan

- Ensures that any work handed out is accompanied by measurements such as target dates, quality expectations, delivery and reporting dates

- Ensures that agreement has been reached on the reasonableness of the work demands with the recipient.

WHY?

The Project Manager must control the sequence of at least the major activities of a stage and when they begin. This ensures that the Project Manager knows what those working on the project are doing, and that the Stage Plan correctly reflects the work and progress.

RESPONSIBILITY

The Project Manager is responsible for the authorisation of Work Packages. The recipient of the Work Package must agree with the targets and constraints before the authorisation can be considered complete. The process 'Managing Product Delivery' (MP) covers the steps of a Team Manager receiving, planning and managing the completion of a Work Package on behalf of a team.

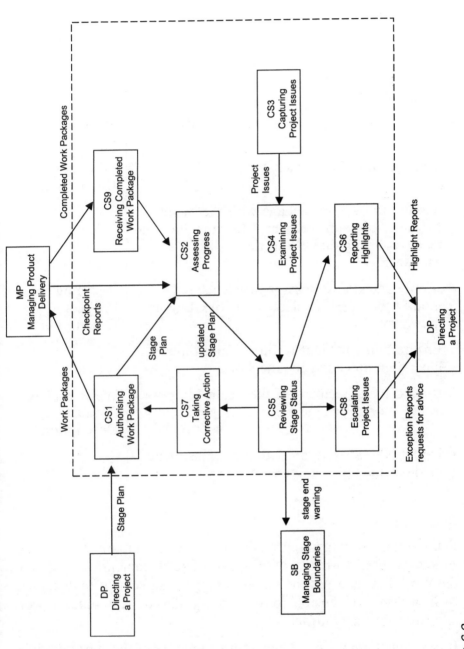

Figure 6.2

HOW?	**LINKS TO OTHER PARTS OF THE BOOK**
• Ensure that there is a Product Description for the work to be done and that this is complete	
• Identify specific quality checking needs	Stage Quality Plan
• Make up the Work Package	Product Description
• Discuss the Work Package with the Team Manager or team member if there is only one team reporting directly to the Project Manager.	
• Jointly assess any risks or problems and modify the Work Package and Risk Log as necessary	Risk Log Product Description
• Ensure that sufficient resources and time have been allocated for the work	
• Record the agreement of the Team Manager in the Work Package	Work Package Product Description
• Update the Stage Plan with any adjustments made as part of the agreement.	

IN PRACTICE

If the Team Manager represents a different company this process should be used formally with appropriate documentation of both the Work Package and the Team Manager's agreement to its targets. In such cases it is sensible to refer specifically to the manner of work allocation in the contract.

If the Stage Plan were to be merely a summary of the start and finish times of major deliverables from a number of teams, there would be a Work Package for each of these major deliverables. There should be definitions in the quality method of the relevant Product Description of who will check the product on behalf of the Project Manager (and/or Project Board) and at which points in the product's development.

If a Team Manager uses contractors to deliver any parts of a Work Package, it is recommended that this is also handled in the same way, i.e. as a Work Package between the Team Manager and the third party.

FOR SMALL PROJECTS

The same process can be used if the work is being allocated to an individual, rather than to a team, but it can be done less formally. The Project Manager should, however, consider if a record is needed for any later appraisal of an individual's performance. Where the Project Manager is also personally performing the work, the process should not be needed.

CS2 – Assessing Progress

WHAT DOES THE PROCESS DO?

- Gathers information to update the Stage Plan to reflect actual progress, effort expended and quality of work carried out.

WHY?

In order to control the stage and make sensible decisions on what, if any, adjustments need to be made, it is necessary to gather information on what has actually happened and be able to compare this against what was planned.

RESPONSIBILITY

The Project Manager is responsible, but may delegate the actual collection of data to Project Support.

How?	Links to OTHER PARTS OF THE BOOK
• Collect Checkpoint Reports	Product Description
• Collect Stage Plan progress information (possibly in the form of timesheets)	
• Obtain estimates on time, cost and effort needed to complete work which is in progress	
• Check whether sufficient resources are available to complete the work as now estimated	
• Check the feedback on quality activities	Quality Log
• Update the Stage Plan with the information	
• Note any potential or real problems.	

In practice

According to the size and environment of the project, the Checkpoint Reports may be written or verbal.

In fixed-price contracts the Project Manager may not be interested in the gathering of costs or the remaining effort of team work, just any changes to estimated completion dates.

For small projects

The Checkpoint Reports may be verbal.

CS3 – Capturing Project Issues

What does the process do?

- Captures, logs and categorises new Project Issues.

WHY?

At any time during the project a problem may occur, a change may be requested or the answer to a question may be sought. If these are missed, it may mean that the project fails to deliver what is required. Alternatively the project may run into some other trouble that could have been foreseen, had the issue been noted at the time it arose. There must be a process to capture these so that they can be presented for the appropriate decision and answer.

RESPONSIBILITY

The Project Manager is responsible. If the project warrants it, help may be given by a Project Support function.

HOW?

	LINKS TO OTHER PARTS OF THE BOOK
• The Project Manager ensures that all possible sources of issues are being monitored	Product Description
• New issues are entered on the Issue Log.	Change Control

IN PRACTICE

A check should be made to ensure that the procedure covers not only requests to change the specification, but also potential failure to meet the specification; potential deviations from objectives or plans; and questions about some aspect of the project which require an answer.

FOR SMALL PROJECTS

Requests for change or failures on the part of the supplier still need to be documented as part of the audit trail of the project.

CS4 – Examining Project Issues

WHAT DOES THE PROCESS DO?

- Analyses each new Project Issue and recommends a course of action

- Reviews each open Project Issue for any change to its circumstances or impact and potentially makes a new recommendation

- Reviews all open Project Issues for any impact on the project risks or the Business Case.

WHY?

Having captured all issues in the process 'Capturing Project Issues' (CS3), these should be examined for impact and the appropriate body for any extra information and decision identified.

RESPONSIBILITY

The Project Manager together with any staff allocated Project Assurance responsibility.

HOW?

	LINKS TO OTHER PARTS OF THE BOOK
- Assemble all pertinent information about the Project Issue	Change Control
- Carry out impact analysis on the technical effort required to resolve the Project Issue	
- Update the Risk Log if the Project Issue reveals a new risk or a change to a known risk	
- Assess whether the Project Issue or its resolution would impact the Business Case	

- Prepare a recommended course of action
- Update the Issue Log with the impact analysis result.

IN PRACTICE

The Project Manager may ask a Team Manager or team member to carry out the analysis, depending on the expertise required. It will be necessary to analyse the financial impact as well as the technical impact. This is part of the Project Assurance role of the Executive. Thought should be given to the time required to do this analysis when designing the project management team, or at least the Executive's Project Assurance role. When producing Stage or Team Plans, an allowance should always be made for the time that the senior specialist people are likely to spend in performing impact analysis on Project Issues. When planning, thought should be given to the likely volume of Project Issues.

FOR SMALL PROJECTS

The Project Manager may be able to carry out impact analysis as soon as the Project Issue is presented and get a decision on the action to take. Thus, in practice, it may be possible to combine the capture and examination processes with the taking of corrective action or the escalation of the Project Issue to the Project Board for decision.

CS5 – Reviewing Stage Status

WHAT DOES THE PROCESS DO?

- Provides a regular reassessment of the status of the stage
- Triggers new work
- Triggers corrective action for any problems
- Provides the information for progress reporting.

WHY?

It is better to check the status of a stage on a regular basis and take action to avoid potential problems than have problems come as a surprise and then have to react to them.

RESPONSIBILITY

The Project Manager, who may seek guidance from the Project Board ('Escalating Project Issues' (CS8)) for any problems that appear to be beyond his/her authority.

HOW?	LINKS TO OTHER PARTS OF THE BOOK
• Review progress against the Stage Plan	
• Review resource and money expenditure	
• Review the impact of any implemented Project Issues on Stage and Project Plans	Change Control
• Check the entries in the Quality Log to ascertain the status of the quality checking	Quality
• Assess if the stage and project will remain within tolerances	Tolerances
• Check the continuing validity of the Business Case	
• Check for changes in the status of any risks	Risk
• Check what work is due to start to ensure that preparations for it are satisfactory	
• Check for any changes external to the project which may impact it.	

IN PRACTICE

The process should be viewed as one that is happening continuously throughout a stage, rather than one that is done, say, every two weeks. Each activity may not need to be done each day, but the Project Manager should ensure that there are sufficient monitoring points (and people allocated to do them) to keep a continuous check. This does not mean that there should always be an instant change of plan in reaction to each slight deviation, but rather an extra monitoring point, a forecast of the potential impact if the situation were to get worse and a tolerance setting at which to trigger remedial work.

A change that affects the Business Case or the risk situation may come at any time. As well as trying to identify such a change as it occurs, it is useful to review the assumptions on which the Business Case and risks are based on a formal, regular basis.

The Project Manager may seek guidance on any Project Issue from the Project Board, and should always do so if there is a threat to the stage or project tolerances.

FOR SMALL PROJECTS

These activities are still required. The Project Manager should make a decision about their frequency according to the project situation and environment.

CS6 – Reporting Highlights

WHAT DOES THE PROCESS DO?

- Produces Highlight Reports for the Project Board.

WHY?

The Project Board needs to be kept informed of project progress if it is to exercise proper control over the project. Rather than have regular progress meetings, reports at regular intervals are recommended between assessments at the end of each stage. The Project Board decides the frequency of the reports at project initiation.

RESPONSIBILITY

The Project Manager is responsible. This process covers the moments when the Project Manager has to stand back and take stock of the situation.

HOW?	LINKS TO OTHER PARTS OF THE BOOK
• Collate the information from any Checkpoint Reports made since the last Highlight Report	'Managing Product Delivery'
• Identify any significant Stage Plan revisions made since the last report	'Assessing Progress'
• Identify current or potential risks to the Business Case	
• Assess the Issue Log for any potential problems which require Project Board attention	Change Control
• Identify any change to other risks	Risk
• Report a summary of this information to the Project Board.	Highlight Report Product Description

IN PRACTICE

Input should come from process CS5 'Reviewing Stage Status'.

The Highlight Report is a formal means of giving a progress update from the Project Manager to the Project Board. It can be used to bring to Project Board attention any failing in resources not under the direct control of the Project Manager and to give early warning of any potential problems that with Project Board attention can be avoided.

The report should be kept brief in order to hold the attention of busy senior management.

It does not prevent informal contact between Project Manager and Project Board if there is an urgent need for information to be passed or advice sought.

FOR SMALL PROJECTS

The Highlight Report need not be in writing if the Project Board agrees to a verbal one.

CS7 – Taking Corrective Action

WHAT DOES THE PROCESS DO?

- Within the limits of the tolerance margins established by the Project Board, the Project Manager takes action to remedy any problems that arise.

WHY?

Failing to take action when the project is drifting away from the Stage Plan invites loss of control.

RESPONSIBILITY

The Project Manager assisted by any Project Support and Project Assurance staff appointed.

HOW?

LINKS TO OTHER PARTS OF THE BOOK

- Ensure that the situation is recorded as a Project Issue

- Ensure that all necessary information about the problem is available

- Identify action options

Change Control

- Evaluate the effort and cost of the options and the impact of the options on the Stage and Project Plans, Business Case and risks

- Select the most appropriate option

- Assess whether it will keep the plans within tolerances

- EITHER implement the corrective actions and update the Stage Plan, if the work is within tolerances

- OR, where it would take the plan beyond tolerance margins, advise the Project Board   'Escalating Project Issues' (CS8)

- The Project Manager may always ask the Project Board for advice informally before deciding on corrective action.

IN PRACTICE

The situation leading to the need to take corrective action should be formally recorded as part of the project audit trail, and the Issue Log is the easiest and most available means of doing this. Many of the reasons for corrective action will be Project Issues raised by other people.

FOR SMALL PROJECTS

It is still important to log why plans were changed.

CS8 – Escalating Project Issues

WHAT DOES THE PROCESS DO?

- Where an issue threatens to go beyond tolerances and the Project Manager feels that he/she cannot take corrective action within the authority limits imposed by the Project Board, the situation must be brought to the attention of the Project Board for advice.

WHY?

Part of the concept of management by exception is that the Project Manager will bring to the immediate attention of the Project Board anything that can be forecast to drive the plan beyond the tolerance limits agreed with the Project Board. This is part of the Project Board staying in overall control.

RESPONSIBILITY

The Project Manager is responsible, assisted by any appointed Project Assurance staff.

HOW?

	LINKS TO OTHER PARTS OF THE BOOK
• Make out an Exception Report to the Project Board, detailing the problem, impact, options and recommendation.	Exception Report Product Description

IN PRACTICE

There are many reasons why the tolerances set for a plan might come under threat. The plan could have been too optimistic, resources may not be performing at expected levels, unexpected activities or events such as illness may have arisen. The opposite may also be true, that the work will finish earlier than the plan's time tolerance or cost less than the budget tolerance.

The most likely cause of a deviation beyond tolerance margins is the work involved in implementing one or more Project Issues. Let's be clear of where a Project Manager stands here. Tolerances are not there to allow the Project Manager (or Team Manager) to 'fit in' change requests. They are there because planning is not an exact science. If the customer wants to add new facilities or change those that were specified, this should lead to the provision of more cash and time from the Project Board. So the Exception Report would say, 'Hey, you've changed your mind. These are the options. This is what it will cost you. Do you want to provide the extra cash and time?'

Another reason for a forecast deviation may be an Off-Specification, some failing of the current solution to meet part of the specification. The onus here is on the Project Manager to find a remedy within the current tolerances. Only if this cannot be done should the Project Manager resort to an Exception Report.

FOR SMALL PROJECTS

The formality of this process will relate to the formality of process CS6, 'Reporting Highlights'. Both will often be informal and brief.

CS9 – Receive Completed Work Package

WHAT DOES THE PROCESS DO?

- This process balances with process MP3, 'Delivering a Work Package'. It records the completion and return of approved Work Packages. The information is passed to process CS2, 'Assessing Progress'.

WHY?

Where work has been recorded as approved to a team or individual, there should be a matching process to record the return of the completed product(s) and its/their acceptance (or otherwise).

RESPONSIBILITY

The Project Manager is responsible, assisted by any appointed Project Support staff.

HOW?	LINKS TO OTHER PARTS OF THE BOOK
• Check the delivery against the requirements of the Work Package	
• Obtain quality confirmation	
• Check that the recipients have accepted the products	
• Ensure that the delivered products have been baselined	Configuration management
• Document any relevant team member appraisal information	
• Pass information about completion to update the Stage Plan.	CS2 'Assessing Progress'

IN PRACTICE

This process is ongoing throughout the stage.

FOR SMALL PROJECTS

The formality of this process will relate to the formality of process CS1, 'Authorising Work Package'. Both will often be informal and brief.

IN PRACTICE

The Project Board should be kept informed of progress and any problems discussed and advice sought via the process DP4, 'Giving Ad Hoc Direction' before presentation of the Stage Plan.

FOR SMALL PROJECTS

The project may be small enough that the Project Plan contains sufficient detail to manage each stage, thus separate Stage Plans are not needed.

<table>
<tr><td>7</td><td># Managing Product Delivery (MP)</td></tr>
</table>

Top Level Diagram

See Figure 7.1.

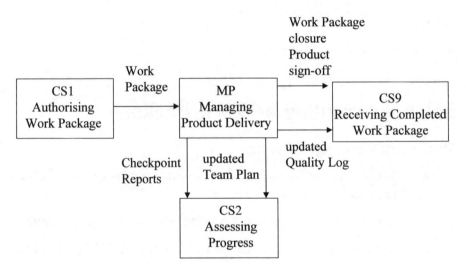

Figure 7.1

WHAT DOES THE PROCESS DO?

- Agrees work requirements with the Project Manager

- Does the work

- Keeps the Project Manager informed on progress, quality and any problems

- Gets approval for the finished work
- Notifies the Project Manager that the work is finished.

WHY?

Where the Project Manager delegates work, there must be appropriate steps by the team or person to whom the work is delegated to indicate understanding and acceptance of the work. While the work is being done, there may be a need to report progress and confirm quality checking. When the work is complete there should be an agreed way of confirming the satisfactory completion.

HOW?

See Figure 7.2.

MP1 – Accepting a Work Package

WHAT DOES THE PROCESS DO?

- Agrees the details of a Work Package with the Project Manager
- Plans the work necessary to complete the Work Package
- Performs the management of risk against the Work Package plan
- Negotiates the time and resource requirements or the target date
- Agrees the quality requirements of the product(s) in the Work Package, the reporting requirements, any tolerance margins or constraints
- Confirms how approval and handover of the finished product(s) is to be done.

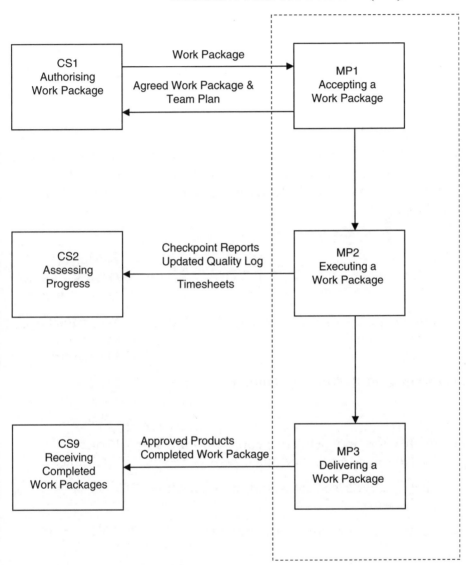

Figure 7.2

WHY?

There must be understanding and agreement between a Team Manager (or an individual) and the Project Manager on any delegated work.

RESPONSIBILITY

Normally the responsibility will lie with a Team Manager to agree a Work Package with the Project Manager. If the person who will do the work reports directly to the Project Manager, then this person would be responsible.

HOW?	LINKS TO OTHER PARTS OF THE BOOK
• Agree with the Project Manager on what is to be delivered	Work Package Product Description
• Ensure that the quality requirements are clear	Product Description (PD)
• Identify any independent people who must be involved in quality checking	Project Assurance
• Identify any target dates and/or constraints for the work	
• Identify any reporting requirements	Checkpoint Report
• Understand how the products of the Work Package are to be handed over when complete	Configuration Management
• Make a plan to do the work	PBP Technique
• Check the plan against the Work Package	

• Adjust the plan or negotiate a change to the Work Package so that the Work Package is achievable	
• Agree suitable tolerance margins for the Work Package.	Controls

IN PRACTICE

Where the Team Manager works for an external contractor, care should be taken to ensure that all the work requirements, as defined above, are understood. A Team Plan for the work will have to be created before the Team Manager can confirm the ability to meet target dates. A Team Manager should avoid pressure from the Project Manager or management within his/her own company to agree to a commitment before checking that the targets can be achieved. This may include confirmation with the Senior Supplier that the necessary resources will be made available.

FOR SMALL PROJECTS

If it is just a single team working directly under the Project Manager, then the CS1–MP1 processes about work that the Project Manager wants to have done will simply be an agreement between the Project Manager and the individual team member. This can either be done formally or informally. The same points need to be covered, but common sense will indicate how much should be documented. The Project Manager should consider whether a record of the work needs to be kept for any future performance appraisal of the individual.

MP2 – Executing a Work Package

WHAT DOES THE PROCESS DO?

• Manages the development/supply of the products/services defined in the Work Package.

WHY?

Having agreed and committed to work in MP1, this process covers the management of that work until its completion.

RESPONSIBILITY

The process is the responsibility of the Team Manager.

HOW?	LINKS TO OTHER PARTS OF THE BOOK
• Allocate work to team members	
• Capture and record the effort expended	
• Monitor progress against the tolerances agreed for the work	
• Monitor and control the risks	Risk
• Evaluate progress and the amount of effort still required to complete the product(s) of the Work Package	
• Feed progress reports back to the Project Manager at the frequency agreed in the Work Package.	Checkpoint Reports
• Ensure that the required quality checks are carried out	
• Ensure that any personnel identified in the Work Package are involved in the quality checking	
• Update the Quality Log with results of all quality checks	Quality
• Raise Project Issues to advise the Project Manager of any problems.	Change Control

IN PRACTICE

Depending on the size of the Work Package, this is a continuous, cyclic process. The emphasis is on being aware of the status of team members' work and keeping the Project Manager up to date on that status.

FOR SMALL PROJECTS

Where the project is too small to have Team Managers, the Project Manager will carry out this process.

MP3 – Delivering a Work Package

WHAT DOES THE PROCESS DO?

- Obtains approval of the products developed/supplied
- Hands over the products to whover is responsible for configuration management
- Advises the Project Manager of the completion of the work.

WHY?

There has to be a process to deliver the requested product(s) and document the agreement that the work has been done satisfactorily.

RESPONSIBILITY

Team Manager.

How?	LINKS TO OTHER PARTS OF THE BOOK
• Confirm that the Quality Log has been updated with details of a successful check on the quality of the product(s)	Quality Log
• Obtain approval from whoever is defined in the Work Package as the end user of the product(s)	
• Transfer the products and control their release to the project's Configuration Librarian	Configuration Management
• Advise the Project Manager that the Work Package is complete	
• Where necessary, obtain a documented appraisal from the Project Manager of the performance in completing the Work Package.	

IN PRACTICE

This can be done formally or informally. The original Work Package should say how it is to be done. The formality usually depends on the criticality of the product and the state of the relationships between the customer and the supplier.

FOR SMALL PROJECTS

This is usually a very simple, informal process of passing the work back to the correct recipient and telling the Project Manager that the work is done. If the team member expects the work to form part of a later appraisal of work, the team member should ensure that the Project Manager documents how well the work was done. The team member should be shown or given a copy of the appraisal.

<table>
<tr><td>**8**</td><td># Managing Stage Boundaries (SB)</td></tr>
</table>

Top Level Diagram

See Figure 8.1

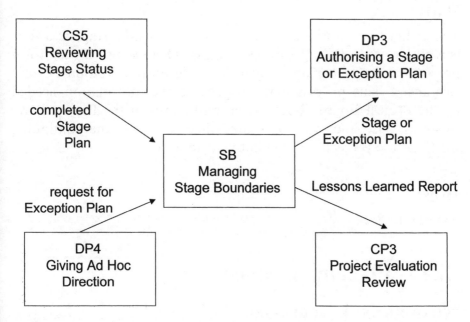

Figure 8.1

WHAT DOES THE PROCESS DO?

- Confirms to the Project Board which products planned to be produced in the current Stage Plan have been delivered

- Gives reasons for the non-delivery of any products which were planned (in the case of deviation forecasts)

- Verifies that any useful lessons learned during the current stage have been recorded in the Lessons Learned Log

- Provides information to the Project Board to allow it to assess the continued viability of the project

- Obtains approval for the next Stage Plan or the Exception Plan

- Ascertains the tolerance margins to be applied to the new plan.

WHY?

The ability to authorise a project to move forward a stage at a time is a major control for the Project Board. There is also a need for a process to create a plan to react to a forecast deviation beyond tolerances. This process aims to provide the information needed by the Project Board about the current status of the Project Plan, Business Case and risks to enable them to judge the continuing worth of the project and commitment to a new plan.

HOW?

See Figure 8.2.

SB1 – Planning a Stage

WHAT DOES THE PROCESS DO?

- Prepares a plan for the next stage.

WHY?

In order to control adequately a stage the Project Manager needs a plan in which the detailed activities go down to the level of a handful of days.

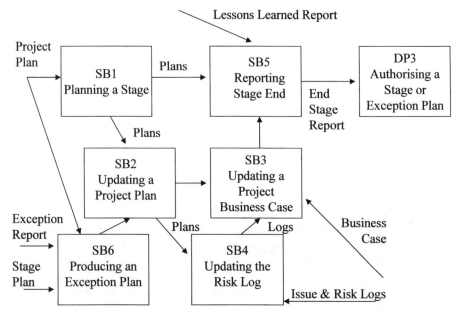

Figure 8.2

RESPONSIBILITY

The Project Manager is responsible, but may get help from Project Support. Any Project Assurance functions should review the plan to ensure products have suitable and timely quality checks with appropriate resources assigned.

HOW?	LINKS TO OTHER PARTS OF THE BOOK
• Check the Project Approach for any guidance on how the products of the next stage are to be produced	
• Check the Issue Log for any issues that will affect the next Stage Plan	Change Control
• Use the common Planning (PL) process to create the draft plan	Planning (PL)

• Document any changes to the personnel of the project management team	Organisation
• Discuss the draft plan with those who have Project Assurance responsibility in order to include Stage Quality Plan requirements	Quality
• Add any formal Quality Reviews and any other quality checks required for Project Assurance purposes	Quality Review
• Identify (as a minimum) the Chairperson of each formal Quality Review	
• Identify with those with Project Assurance responsibility the required Reviewers for each formal quality check	Stage Quality Plan
• Ensure that the plan includes all required management products	Product-based Planning
• Check the plan for any new or changed risks and update the Risk Log	Risk
• Modify the plan, if necessary, in the light of the risk analysis.	

SB2 – Updating a Project Plan

WHAT DOES THE PROCESS DO?

  • The Project Plan is updated with the actual costs and schedule from the stage that has just finished, plus the estimated cost and schedule of the next Stage Plan.

WHY?

As one stage is completed and the next one planned, the Project Plan must be updated so that the Project Board has the most up-to-date information on likely project costs and a schedule on which to partially base its decision on whether the project is still a viable business proposition.

Responsibility

The Project Manager is responsible, but may have help from Project Support.

How?	Links to other parts of the book
• Ensure that the current Stage Plan has been updated with final costs and dates	CS2
• Create a new version of the Project Plan ready to be updated	Configuration Management
• Update the Project Plan with the actual costs and dates of the current stage	
• Update the Project Plan with the estimated costs, resource requirements and dates of the next stage	
• Update any later stages of the Project Plan on the basis of any relevant information made available since the last update	
• Check to see if events mean that the Project Approach has to be modified.	SU5

In practice

Text should be added to the new version, explaining why any changes have occurred. This is an important part of the Project Manager's audit trail of documents covering the management of the project.

For small projects

All the activity detail may be in the Project Plan with no separate Stage Plans. The Project Plan should be updated with the information described above.

SB3 – Updating a Project Business Case

WHAT DOES THE PROCESS DO?

- Modifies the Business Case, where appropriate, on the basis of information from the current stage and the plan for the next stage.

WHY?

The whole project should be business driven, so the Project Board should review a revised Business Case as a major part of the check on the continued viability of the project.

RESPONSIBILITY

The Project Manager and whoever has responsibility for the business assurance for the project.

HOW?

	LINKS TO OTHER PARTS OF THE BOOK
• Create a new version of the Business Case ready to be updated	Configuration Management
• Review the expected costs in the investment appraisal against the new forecast in the updated Project Plan	
• Review the financial benefits in the investment appraisal against any new forecasts	Business Case
• Review the reasons in the Business Case and check that there has been no change or that no new reasons have come to light	
• Modify the new version of the Business Case in the light of any changes to forecast.	

IN PRACTICE

The Business Case should be reviewed **minimally** at each stage end, but more frequently if the stages are long or the Business Case is at all at risk.

FOR SMALL PROJECTS

It should not be assumed that the Business Case is unimportant for a small project.

SB4 – Updating the Risk Log

WHAT DOES THE PROCESS DO?

- Checks the known risks to project success for any change to their circumstances and looks for any new risks.

WHY?

Part of the assessment of the project's viability is an examination of the likelihood and impact of potential risks.

RESPONSIBILITY

The Project Manager collates the information on risks, but each known risk should have been allocated to an 'owner', the person best placed to monitor that risk.

HOW?

- Ensure that the Risk Log is up to date with the latest information on the identified risks

- Ensure that any new risks identified in creating the next Stage Plan have been entered on the Risk Log

LINKS TO OTHER PARTS OF THE BOOK

Risk

- Assess all open risks to the project, as defined in the Risk Log

- Decide if the next Stage Plan needs to be modified to avoid, reduce or monitor risks

- Create contingency plans for any serious risks that cannot be avoided or reduced to manageable proportions.

IN PRACTICE

An assessment of the risks should be part of the End Stage Report. In practice, the Project Manager should informally discuss any serious risks with the Project Board so that the risk situation and any extra costs incurred in reacting to those risks do not come as a surprise at the end stage assessment.

FOR SMALL PROJECTS

Continuous risk assessment and management are important to all levels of project.

SB5 – Reporting Stage End

WHAT DOES THE PROCESS DO?

- Reports on the results of the current stage

- Forecasts the time and resource requirements of the next stage, if applicable

- Looks for a Project Board decision on the future of the project.

WHY?

Normally the Project Board manages by exception and therefore only needs to meet if things are forecast to deviate beyond tolerance levels. But as part of its control the Project Board only gives approval to the Project Manager to undertake one stage at a time, at the end of which it reviews the anticipated benefits, costs, time-scale and risks and makes a decision whether to continue with the project or not.

RESPONSIBILITY

The Project Manager is responsible.

HOW?	LINKS TO OTHER PARTS OF THE BOOK
• Report on the actual costs and time of the current stage and measure these against the plan that was approved by the Project Board	End Stage Report Product Description
• Report on the impact of the current stage's costs and time taken on the Project Plan	
• Report on any impact from the current stage's results on the Business Case	
• Report on the status of the Issue Log	Change Control
• Report on the extent and results of the quality work done in the current stage	Quality Log
• Provide details of the next Stage Plan (if applicable)	
• Identify any necessary revisions to the Project Plan caused by the next Stage Plan	
• Identify any changes to the Business Case caused by the next Stage Plan	
• Report on the risk situation	
• Recommend the next action (e.g. approval of the next Stage Plan).	

IN PRACTICE

The Project Board should be aware of what will be in the End Stage Report before it formally receives it.

FOR SMALL PROJECTS

The report may be verbal, if this has the agreement of the Project Board.

IN PRACTICE

The Project Board should be kept informed of progress and any problems discussed and advice sought via the process DP4, 'Giving Ad Hoc Direction' before presentation of the Stage Plan.

FOR SMALL PROJECTS

The project may be small enough that the Project Plan contains sufficient detail to manage each stage, thus separate Stage Plans are not needed.

SB6 – Producing an Exception Plan

WHAT DOES THE PROCESS DO?

- At the request of the Project Board the Project Manager prepares a new plan to replace the remainder of the current plan in response to an Exception Report.

WHY?

The Project Board approves a Stage Plan on the understanding that it stays within its defined tolerance margins. When an Exception Report indicates that the current tolerances are likely to be exceeded, the Project Board may ask for a new plan to reflect the changed situation and which can be controlled within newly specified tolerance margins.

RESPONSIBILITY

The Project Manager is responsible in consultation with the Project Assurance function.

HOW?	LINKS TO OTHER PARTS OF THE BOOK
• An Exception Plan has exactly the same format as the plan it replaces	Plans
• An Exception Plan covers the time from the present moment to the end of the current plan.	SB1

IN PRACTICE

Reasons for the deviation forecast can be many, such as:

- Work on approved requests for change cannot be done within current tolerances

- The supplier has discovered that it cannot supply part of the solution

- The stage cannot deliver all its products within the current tolerances.

FOR SMALL PROJECTS

There is the temptation not to replan, but only to 'remember' that changes have occurred. It is, however, important to advise the Project Board of any potential deviation beyond tolerances, to have a record that the Stage Plan was changed to accommodate the change **and that the Project Board approved** the new targets.

The same concept can be applied to Team Plans if they are forecast to deviate beyond tolerances.

9 | Closing a Project (CP)

Top-Level Diagram

See Figure 9.10.

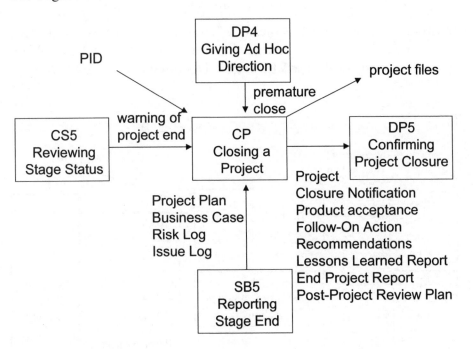

Figure 9.1

What does the process do?

- Checks that all required products have been delivered and accepted

- Checks that all Project Issues have been dealt with
- Records any recommendations for subsequent work on the product
- Passes on any useful lessons learned during the project
- Recommends closure of the project to the Project Board
- Plans to measure the achievement of the project's Business Case.

WHY?

Every project should come to a controlled completion.

In order to have its success measured, a project must be brought to a close when the Project Manager believes that it has met the objectives set out in the Project Initiation Document.

HOW?

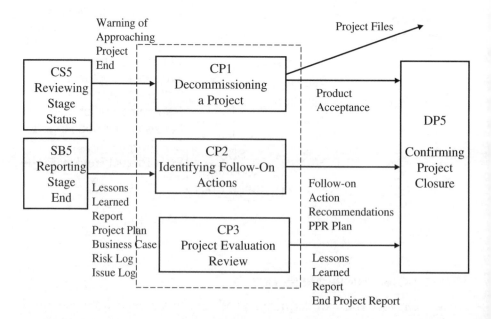

Figure 9.2

CP1 – Decommissioning the Project

WHAT DOES THE PROCESS DO?

- Gets agreement from the customer that the acceptance criteria have been met

- Confirms acceptance of the project's products from the customer and those who will support the product during its operational life

- Checks that all Project Issues are closed

- Arranges archiving for the project files.

WHY?

The customer and supplier must agree that a project has met its objectives before it can close.

There must be a check that there are no outstanding problems or requests.

The project documentation, particularly agreements and approvals, should be preserved for any later audits.

RESPONSIBILITY

The Project Manager and any Project Support staff assigned to the project.

HOW?

LINKS TO OTHER PARTS OF THE BOOK

- Check that all Project Issues have been closed

  Change Control

- Get the customer's agreement that the acceptance criteria have been met

  SU

- Ensure that all products have been completed and accepted by the customer

- Ensure that, where applicable, those who will be responsible for maintenance and support of the products are ready to accept the product

  Configuration Management

- Complete and archive the project files.

IN PRACTICE

This process may be abridged if the Project Board brings the project to a premature close. There will need to be a carefully managed handover of the products between the project and operational and/or support staff unless one central group handles configuration management methods for both parts of the product's lifespan – development and use.

If any acceptance criteria have not been fully met, the customer and supplier may agree to record this as a Project Issue (Off-Specification) to be dealt with in a later project.

The final product may be handed over to a new third party to operate and maintain, and there may be contractual arrangements involved in the acceptance of the product.

FOR SMALL PROJECTS

Notification of the release of resources may be very informal, if required at all.

CP2 – Identifying Follow-on Actions

WHAT DOES THE PROCESS DO?

- Identifies any work that should be done following the project
- Prepares a plan for when the realisation of the project's expected benefits should be checked.

WHY?

Any knowledge of unfinished business at the end of a project should be documented, checked with the Project Board and passed to the appropriate body for action.

RESPONSIBILITY

The Project Manager is responsible. Input should be sought from any Project Assurance roles used.

# How?	LINKS TO OTHER PARTS OF THE BOOK
• Check for any omissions in the product against the Project Definition in the PID or suggestions on how to improve the product	
• Ensure that any omissions and suggestions are recorded as Project Issues	Change Control
• Check the Issue Log for any Project Issues that were not completed or rejected	
• Check the Risk Log for any risks that may affect the product in its operational life	Risk
• Draw up Follow-on Action Recommendations and cross-refer the entry in the Issue or Risk Log	Follow-on Action Recommendations Product Description
• Identify when measurement can be made of whether the product has delivered its benefits, and prepare a plan to carry out that measurement.	Post-Project Review plan

IN PRACTICE

The timing and arrangements for any Post-Project Review should be discussed with the Project Board, particularly where there is an external supplier or support group.

Where the project is part of a programme, any recommendations for follow-on actions should be passed via the Project Board to the programme management.

Where the project is part of a programme, the project's work may have been purely in support of the programme's Business Case, so there may be no requirement for a Post-Project Review.

FOR SMALL PROJECTS

There may be no requirement by the Senior User for a Post-Project Review.

CP3 – Project Evaluation Review

WHAT DOES THE PROCESS DO?

- Assesses the project's results against its objectives
- Provides statistics on the performance of the project
- Records useful lessons that were learned.

WHY?

One way in which to improve the quality of project management is to learn from the lessons of past projects.

As part of closing the project, the Project Board needs to assess the performance of the project and the Project Manager. This may also form part of the customer's appraisal of a supplier, to see if the contract has been completed, or to see if that supplier should be used again.

RESPONSIBILITY

The Project Manager, Project Support and any Project Assurance roles used.

HOW?	LINKS TO OTHER PARTS OF THE BOOK
• Write the End Project Report, evaluating the management, quality and technical methods, tools and processes used	End Project Report
• Examine the Risk Log and actions taken and record any useful comments	Risk
• Examine the Issue Log and actions taken and record any useful comments	Change Control
• Examine the Quality Log and record any useful comments	Quality
• Turn the Lessons Learned Log into a Lessons Learned Report.	Lessons Learned Report (PD)

IN PRACTICE

The Lessons Learned Log should have been updated throughout the project.

If there are suggestions that the quality management system used by the project needs modification, it should be made clear that such comments are directed to the appropriate quality assurance function.

FOR SMALL PROJECTS

The Project Board may not require an extensive End Project Report.

10 | Planning (PL)

Top Level Diagram

See Figure 10.1.

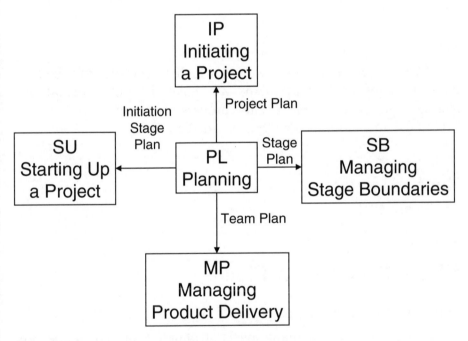

Figure 10.1

WHAT DOES THE PROCESS DO?

- Defines the levels of plan needed for the project

- Decides what planning tools and estimating methods will be used

- Identifies the products whose delivery has to be planned

- Identifies the activities needed to deliver those products and the dependencies between them

- Estimates the effort needed for each activity

- Allocates the activities to resources and schedules the activities against a timeframe

- Analyses the risks inherent in the plan

- Adds explanatory text to the final plan.

WHY?

PRINCE2 offers a standard way in which to produce any level of plan. This means that all plans will have the same format and method of development. The process is based around the PRINCE2 technique of Product-based Planning.

HOW?

See Figure 10.2.

PL1 – Designing a Plan

WHAT DOES THE PROCESS DO?

- Decides on how many levels of plan are needed by the project

- Identifies any planning tools to be used

- Identifies the method(s) of estimating to be used.

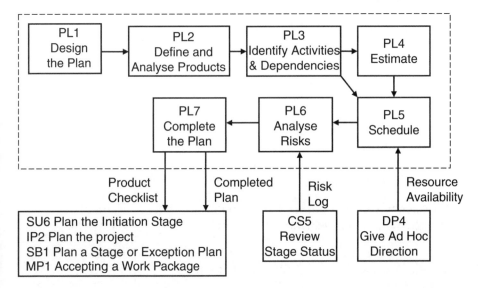

Figure 10.2

WHY?

This process is carried out only once per project, the first time that the **Planning** process is used. It defines the standards to be used in all future plans. The result should be a consistent set of plans.

RESPONSIBILITY

The Project Manager.

HOW?

- Decide on what levels of plan are needed for the project, i.e. Project Plan, Stage Plans, Team Plans

- Ascertain if the organisation or programme uses a particular planning tool as standard

LINKS TO OTHER PARTS OF THE BOOK

Plans

• Identify the planning tool to be used in the Project Plan, part of the Project Initiation Document	Project Initiation Document
• Identify what estimating method(s) are available and suitable for the project	
• Ensure that the estimating method(s) chosen contain allowances for Project Issue analysis, telephone calls, ad hoc meetings, learning curves, experience, etc.	
• Discuss with the Project Board whether there should be a Change Budget set aside	Project Controls
• Discuss with the Project Board whether there should be a separate allowance for any anticipated Contingency Plans.	Risk

IN PRACTICE

Where the project is part of a programme, the programme will have made most of these decisions, and it is just a question of finding out what the standards are. Beware of allocating any resource, especially yourself, 100 per cent of its time to an activity. No one is 100 per cent efficient. There will inevitably be interruptions such as telephone calls, ad hoc meetings and non-project work that demand your time. These should be allowed for in your estimate of how much time people can commit to the work in your plan. Even the most efficient experienced workers is unlikely to devote more than 70 per cent of their time to planned work. At least 50 per cent of a Project Manager's time should be spent in managing. The Project Manager of a large project should not contemplate doing any of the specialist work at all.

FOR SMALL PROJECTS

A really small project may not need a planning tool, but a little thought should be given to the other steps before diving in and assuming you can hold it all in your head. The comments about how efficient people are still holds true for the smallest project.

PL2 – Defining and Analysing Products

WHAT DOES THE PROCESS DO?

- Identifies the products whose delivery has to be planned

- Describes each of the products in terms of purpose, composition and quality criteria and ensures that these descriptions are agreed by all concerned

- Identifies the sequence of delivering the products and the dependencies between them.

WHY?

By defining the products and their quality requirements everyone can see and understand the required plan result. It means that whoever has to deliver a product knows in advance what its purpose is, to what quality it has to be built and what interfaces there are with other products.

RESPONSIBILITY

The planner is responsible. This will be either the Project Manager or a Team Manager, depending on the type of plan being produced. The users of any of the products to be delivered within the plan should be involved in writing the Product Descriptions, particularly in defining the quality criteria.

HOW?

LINKS TO OTHER PARTS OF THE BOOK

Product-based Planning

- Identify the products required

- Write Product Descriptions for them
- Draw a diagram showing the sequence of delivery and dependencies between the products

- Optionally produce a Product Checklist. | Product Checklist

IN PRACTICE

This is a key point in PRINCE2. If you are not doing this step, then you are not really using PRINCE2. It is an ideal method of involving users, specialists and Project Assurance roles in the creation of a plan, without the normal problems of 'design by committee'.

FOR SMALL PROJECTS

It is very tempting in small projects to assume that use of Product-based Planning is not needed. Experience has shown me that it is very easy to forget a product, do things in the wrong order or fail to consider a quality requirement when you dive in and 'just do it'. It doesn't take much time to do this step and it will always pay dividends.

PL3 – Identifying Activities and Dependencies

WHAT DOES THE PROCESS DO?

- Identifies all activities necessary to deliver the products
- Defines the dependencies between the activities.

WHY?

For Stage and Team Plans the Product Flow Diagram (created in process PL2) may still be at too high a level for the purposes of estimation and control. This optional process allows a further breakdown, based on the PFD, until each activity will last only a handful of days.

RESPONSIBILITY

The planner is responsible. This will be either the Project Manager or a Team Manager, depending on the type of plan being produced.

How?

- Consider if a product in the PFD is too big to estimate or would need such a large effort that it would be difficult to control against that estimate

  Product-based Planning technique

- Where a product is too big, break it down into the activities needed to produce it. This should continue down to the level where an activity is less than ten days' effort, ideally no more than five days

- Where a product has been broken down into several activities, put the activities into their correct sequence

- Review the dependencies between products and refine them to give dependencies between the new activities. For example, where PFD dependencies went from the end of one product to the start of the next, is there now an opportunity to overlap, or start some activities on a product before all the activities on its preceding product have been done?

In practice

You may decide not to do this step, but simply extend the previous step, i.e. continue thinking about products, rather than activities, down to the level where you have all the detail you need for your plan. This step was originally included because all planning tools used Work Breakdown Structures and assumed you would be working with activities and tasks. This process was inserted as a bridge from PRINCE2's product approach. Other people found it convenient to use this process to draw a line below which Product Descriptions were not needed.

FOR SMALL PROJECTS

Following the above comments this process may not be needed for a small plan. The previous step may give enough detail for estimation and control.

PL4 – Estimating

WHAT DOES THE PROCESS DO?

- Identifies the types of resource needed for the plan

- Estimates the effort for each activity/product.

WHY?

The objective is to identify the resources and effort required to complete each activity or product.

RESPONSIBILITY

The planner. This will be either the Project Manager or Team Manager. Possibly there will be expert help available from Project Support.

HOW?

LINKS TO
OTHER PARTS
OF THE BOOK

- Examine each activity/product and identify what resource types it requires. Apart from human resources there may be other resources needed, such as equipment

- With human resources, consider and document what level of skill you are basing the estimate on

- Judge what level of efficiency you will base your estimates on, what allowance for non-project time you will need to use

- Estimate the effort needed for each activity/ product

- Understand whether that is an estimate of uninterrupted work, to which the allowances must be added, or whether the estimate already includes allowances

- Document any assumptions you have made, e.g. the use of specific named resources, levels of skill and experience, the availability of user resources when you need them. Check the assumptions with those who have such knowledge, such as the Senior Supplier and Senior User.

IN PRACTICE

The organisation may already have estimating guidelines for standard types of product. This should be particularly true for standard PRINCE2 management products. For example, the amount of time to write an End Stage Report, Highlight Report, and to prepare and hold a quality review should be known.

FOR SMALL PROJECTS

Beware of giving an estimate for the project before you have gone through this process. It seems easy to give a figure off the top of your head for a small project. But once given, the Project Board will hold you to this. It is amazing how many forgotten activities, unchecked assumptions and thoughts of people being 100 per cent effective lie waiting to be discovered by this process even in even the smallest of projects.

PL5 – Scheduling

WHAT DOES THE PROCESS DO?

- Matches resources to activities/products

- Schedules work according to sequence and dependencies

- Adjusts the schedule to avoid people being over- or under-used

- Negotiates a solution with the Project Board for problems such as too few resources, too many resources or inability to meet fixed target dates

- Calculates the cost of the resources used in the plan.

WHY?

A plan can only show whether it can meet its targets when the activities are put together in a schedule against a timeframe, showing when activities will be done and by what resources.

RESPONSIBILITY

The Project Manager.

HOW?

- Draw a planning network
- Assess resource availability. This should include dates of availability as well as what the scale of that availability is. Any known information on holidays and training courses should be gathered
- Allocate activities to resources and produce a draft schedule
- Revise the draft to remove as many peaks and troughs in resource usage as possible
- Add in management activities or products (Stage and Team Plans only)
- Calculate resource utilisation and costs.

LINKS TO OTHER PARTS OF THE BOOK

IN PRACTICE

This may be the point when you transfer the plan to your planning tool.

FOR SMALL PROJECTS

You may not need a planning tool. You should remember to add time and effort for any management products.

PL6 – Analysing Risks

WHAT DOES THE PROCESS DO?

- Checks the draft plan for any risks in it.

WHY?

You should not commit to a plan without considering what risks are involved in it and what impact the plan might have on risks already known.

RESPONSIBILITY

The planner is responsible. This will be either the Project Manager or a Team Manager, depending on the type of plan being produced.

HOW?

LINKS TO OTHER PARTS OF THE BOOK

- Look for any external dependencies. These always represent one or more risks. Products from other projects might not arrive on time. They might be of poor quality or be wrong in some other way

- Look for any assumptions you have made in the plan, e.g. the resources available to you. Each assumption is a risk

- Look at each resource in the plan. Is there a risk involved? For example, that a new resource doesn't perform at the expected level, or that a resource's availability is not achieved

- Are the tools or technology unproven?

- Take the appropriate risk actions. Where appropriate, revise the plan. Make sure that any new or modified risks are shown in the Risk Log.

Risk

FOR SMALL PROJECTS

Where the project is too small to have Team Managers, the Project Manager will carry out this process.

PL7 – Completing a Plan

WHAT DOES THE PROCESS DO?

- Adds text to explain the plan.

WHY?

A plan in diagrammatic form is not self-explanatory. It needs text.

RESPONSIBILITY

The planner is responsible. This will be either the Project Manager or a Team Manager, depending on the type of plan being produced.

How?	Links to other parts of the book
• Agree tolerance levels for the plan	Project Controls
• Document the expected working environment, what work the plan covers, the approach to the work and how the quality of its products will be checked	
• Document any assumptions you have made	
• Add the planning dates to the Product Checklist (if used)	PL2
• Publish the plan.	

In practice

The majority of the material for the text will evolve from the previous planning steps. Some of it will already be known because of local standards.

For small projects

Even if you don't have to publish a plan, you should still document the assumptions.

11	**Business Case**

Philosophy

Every project should be driven by a business need. If it has no justification in terms of the business, it should not be undertaken.

The Business Case is a vital project management tool. It should be considered before any project is commissioned, ideally at a higher level such as the strategy group, and certainly as part of any feasibility study.

- A high level Business Case should be included in the Project Mandate. If it is not, then one should be added as part of developing the Project Brief.

- The contents of a Business Case should include the reasons for the project, the prioritised business benefits, the options considered, costs of the proposed solution, a cost/benefit analysis, a GAP (Good, Average and Poor) analysis and a sensitivity analysis. The last two are explained in a little more detail later in the chapter. A summary of the major risks may be included from the Risk Log for readers who may not see the whole PID.

- Well-constructed Business Cases will have assessed the impact of doing nothing and will identify the differences achieved by implementing the proposed solution.

The Business Case should be formally reviewed at the start of a project, and again at stage boundaries and at project closure. It should also be reviewed when major change requests are made. It should be monitored continuously throughout the project.

If a project is part of a larger programme, its justification will point at the Business Case of the programme. In such a case, the project may have no business justification itself, but contribute to achievement of the programme Business Case. In this case, the reviews mentioned above will refer back to the continuing need for the project within the perceived needs for the programme.

Overview

This chapter will describe the content of the Business Case and establish the need to review the Business Case as a major exercise at the start of the project and on an ongoing basis throughout the project.

Detail

The Business Case contains the following components.

REASONS

This is a narrative description of the justification for undertaking the project. This may have been initially defined in a feasibility study (where one has been done), and should ideally describe the reasons why the system is needed. This may be the only information available until the Business Case is revised as part of project initiation.

BENEFITS

A narrative description of what the expected benefits are, plus estimated benefit figures over the life of the product. It is important to look ahead to the judgement of whether benefits have been achieved after the end of the project. Benefits should be defined in terms that are:

- Measurable at the start of the project
- Measurable when the final product is in use.

OPTIONS CONSIDERED

This should be a summary of any Project Approaches considered, together with the reasons that led to selection of the final option.

COST AND TIMESCALE

This gives the estimated development and running costs for the project and the expected delivery date.

INVESTMENT APPRAISAL

Accountants use the Investment Appraisal to illustrate what the cost/benefit balance will look like over time; but what do we use as a baseline when expressing benefits?

By way of answering this question, consider what would happen if the project was not done – none of the costs would be incurred and the benefits would not be accrued. This is known as the 'do nothing' option and is used as the benchmark against which the predicted costs and benefits are measured.

THE 'DO NOTHING' OPTION

In every Business Case the 'do nothing' option should be considered. Indeed in a lot of cases it is the 'do nothing' option that justifies the need for change and hence the project.

Examples of this are where the 'do nothing' options results in:

- The loss of market share
- Large maintenance costs
- Heavy legal penalties for non-conformance to law.

It is important to remember that the 'do nothing' option should be calculated by assessing the implications of staying with the current mode of operation for the anticipated life of the new product/service/system. It should be calculated from the planned date of the start of the proposed project for the expected life of the new/replacement product, with estimates for inflation and cost increase included.

THE 'DO SOMETHING' OPTION

Estimates of the implications of implementing the project's solution need to be made in a similar way and over a similar time period to the 'do nothing' option above. The effects on running costs and benefits need to be assessed. It is not relevant here to go into lengthy discussion on benefit quantification. Suffice to say that an effective Business Case is one that gives the most accurate estimate of **direct** benefit resulting from implementation.

So-called **intangible** benefits should be excluded as these tend to indicate the existence of a higher level programme or portfolio Business Case. If no direct benefit results (including reduced costs) then this indicates that, on its own, the project does not have a Business Case. In this instance it can only be contributing to a higher level case, or is simply not economically viable!

Project Managers often make the mistake, when developing or refining the Business Case, of quantifying benefit and cost implications themselves. This is not usually wise. Costs and benefits are only estimates and it is important to get 'experts' to provide these estimates. It is the role of the Project Manager to seek out the 'experts' and ensure their involvement. It is sensible to get the users to quantify benefits. They may need a little help from you, but the figures should be recognised as theirs. When the product's real benefits are finally measured, you don't want the user accusing you of overestimating its value.

The assessment of benefits (and reduced costs) should follow a natural path. Projects have objectives that when achieved, realise benefits. In order to meet objectives, detailed requirements have to be identified and met. Solutions are built to meet these requirements, which will, in turn, achieve the objectives and hence realise the benefits. The implementation and operation of the solution start to deliver the benefits. Maintaining this link, throughout the project, is a vital task in refining the Business Case.

CASH FLOW

The Business Case is calculated by establishing the difference between the 'do something' option and the 'do nothing' option and comparing this with the investment cost required for the project.

The most straightforward way of expressing this is via the cash flow model.

Each organisation has its own standards, but they are all loosely based on the concept of a cash flow model. A simple table to illustrate this would assume a development period of one year (year 0) and a system life of four years (years 1 to 4). The table would have four 'rows' or entry lines.

The costs row within the table then represents the development costs in year 0 and the predicted running costs of the delivered system over years 1 through 4.

The benefits row represents the benefits predicted from the operation of the delivered system. The net benefits row represents the benefits minus the costs for each year. The cash flow row is the cumulative running total of the net benefits.

	Yr 0	Yr 1	Yr 2	Yr 3	Yr 4
Costs	60	5	5	5	5
Benefits	0	20	25	30	25
Net Benefits	−60	15	20	25	20
Cash Flow	−60	−45	−25	0	20

This is about the simplest possible representation of a cost/benefit analysis.

The problem with this example is that it does not account for the 'time value of money'. This concept states that money received in the future is not as useful as money received today, therefore it must be considered as being worth less.

If you were asked whether you would rather have £100 now or £100 this time next year, the answer will probably be 'Now'. Why? Because it could be invested in order to gain interest, or it could be used to buy something that will cost more next year.

How much interest depends on the interest rate being used. If an interest rate of 6 per cent is assumed, then giving someone £1.06 one year from now is equivalent to giving them £1 now. Equally, it can be said that giving someone £1 next year is equivalent to giving them 94p now. Thus the discount factor (as it is known) is, in this case, 0.94.

This 'discounting factor' is arrived at by the following formula:

$$\frac{1}{(1 + i)^n}$$

where 'i' is the interest rate used – e.g. 0.06 – and 'n' is the number of years hence.

Every organisation has a standard interest rate that they use and it is usually held in the finance department. The finance department will also hold tables of discount rates against various numbers of years and interest rates. This avoids the necessity for working them out. (If a rough estimate is required, just use the current bank loan rate.)

NET PRESENT VALUE

Discounting can be incorporated into a cash flow model.

Each net benefits value is multiplied by the appropriate discount factor to arrive at the discounted net benefits.

Application of discounting can reduce the NPV (Net Present Value) of a benefit quite substantially over a period of time. If we take the example above and apply a discount of 6 per cent, the cumulative profit after four years reduces from 20 to 8.7.

	Yr 0	Yr 1	Yr 2	Yr 3	Yr 4
Costs	60	5	5	5	5
Benefits	0	20	25	30	25
Net Benefits	−60	15	20	25	20
Discount Factor	1	0.94	0.89	0.84	0.79
Discounted Benefit	−60	14.1	17.8	21.0	15.8
Net Present Value	−60	−45.9	−28.1	−7.1	+8.7

Another way of expressing the time value of money is through Internal Rate of Return (IRR).

INTERNAL RATE OF RETURN

As the interest rate used to calculate NPV gets higher, there comes a point where there is an interest rate that would give an NPV of zero over the period of time given.

That rate is known as the Internal Rate of Return (IRR), and is used to compare one project with another (to see which is the better investment), and against the company standard (to see whether the money could be put to a better use). IRR can be understood as follows. If all of the money for the project development was borrowed, and the project broke even, then the interest rate paid on that borrowed money would be the IRR.

If IRR is used, then the accountants will have a formula, or more likely a spreadsheet model, to calculate it. What is required to calculate it is an interest rate that gives a positive NPV, and one that gives a negative one, along with the values of those NPVs derived.

GAP AND SENSITIVITY

It must always be remembered that the figures we are using for costs and benefits are all estimated. One way of assessing the robustness of the Business Case is by using GAP Analysis.

GAP (Good, Average, Poor) is sometimes better known as Best, Most likely, Worst cases. It can be calculated by taking into consideration allowances for estimating inaccuracies; building in tolerances; and allowing for the impact of risks (see below). In a well-managed project the Business Case GAP will narrow as the project progresses and more certainty is established. The wider the GAP the more the uncertainty and risk of the project. Refining the Business Case GAP is an important activity throughout the project.

However, sensitivity analysis is an even more valuable activity in that it can pinpoint the areas of the project that are highly sensitive and hence the ones that need closer management and control. A highly sensitive Business Case is indicating great project risk and a need for rigorous change management. Sensitivity needs to be reviewed and refined throughout the project.

MAJOR RISKS

In some environments, particularly government, there may be an expectation of seeing a section on risks in the Business Case, even though there is a section on risk in the PID. If this is required, it can be a summary of the Risk Log.

Links

As mentioned earlier, a basic Business Case should appear in the Project Mandate, or be developed as part of 'Preparing a Project Brief' (SU4).

There is a major link with the initiation stage, in which the Project Board should review the Business Case before it decides whether the project should be undertaken.

The Business Case should be reviewed at the end of each stage in SB4, 'Updating the Business Case'. This forms part of the end stage assessment, which is reviewed by the Project Board in DP3, 'Authorising a Stage or Exception Plan', as part of its decision on whether to continue with the project.

The impact on the Business Case is assessed for each major Project Issue as part of the process CS4, 'Examining Project Issues'.

Achievement of the Business Case will be finally judged in the Post-Project Review some time after the project has finished.

Do's and Don'ts

Do examine the Business Case if those who will use the final product put it up. Be sure that the Business Case figures are genuine, not just pulled out of the air. Many impressive Business Cases are put up to endorse a political wish or whim, but they do not stand up to close scrutiny.

If you are the supplier, beware of the temptation to write the customer's Business Case. The customer has to 'own' the Business Case. The customer may need some help in thinking in financial terms of how to justify the project, but if the project should run into cash trouble, you don't want the customer saying 'But you said it was justifiable.'

If it's a Large Project

The Business Case is likely to take some time to prepare. There should have been at least the outline of a Business Case in the Project Mandate that triggered the project. It is likely that there was a feasibility study that should contain a Business Case.

If it's a Small Project

Don't ignore the philosophy that there should be business justification for every project. A lot of small projects undertaken without business justification can waste as much as one large project. It may be satisfactory to carry out a short, informal Business Case appraisal, but the Executive should still be convinced that a genuine Business Case exists.

12 | Project Organisation

Philosophy

The organisation for any project should be based on a customer/supplier relationship. The customer is the person or group who wants the end product, specifies what it should be and, usually, pays for the development of that product. The supplier is whoever provides the resources to build or procure the end product. This is true even if the customer and supplier work for the same company. If this is the case they may still, for example, report to different lines of management, have different budgets and therefore have a different view of the finances of the project. The customer will be asking, 'Will the end product save me money or bring in a profit?' The supplier will be asking if the providing of appropriate resources will earn a profit.

Establishing an effective organisational structure for the project is crucial to its success. Every project needs direction, management, control and communication. Before you start any project you should establish what the project organisation is to be. You need to ask the questions **even if it is a very small project**. Answers to these questions will separate the real decision makers from those who have opinions, identify responsibility and accountability, and establish a structure for communication. Examples of the questions to ask are:

- Who is providing the funds?
- Who has the authority to say what is needed?
- Who is providing the development resources?

- Who will manage the project on a day-to-day basis?

- How many different sets of specialist skills are needed?

- Who will establish and maintain the required standards?

- Who will safeguard the developed products?

- Who will know where all the documents are?

- What are the limits to the Project Manager's authority and who sets those limits?

A project needs a different organisation structure to line management. It needs to be more flexible and is likely to require a broad base of skills for a comparatively short period of time. A project is often cross-functional and may need to combine people working full time on the project with others who have to divide their time between the project and other duties. The Project Manager may have direct management control over some of the project staff, but may also have to manage staff that report to another management structure.

The management structure of the customer will very often be different to that of the supplier. They will have different priorities, different interests to protect, but in some way they must be united in the common aims of the project.

Four Layers of Management

See Figure 12.1.

The PRINCE2 philosophy, when designing what the project organisation should be, is to consider four layers of management. According to the size and importance of the project, you may not need all four to be represented, but that should be a decision you take when you understand the philosophy and can compare it to the needs of a specific project.

LAYER THREE

Layer three is the Project Manager role, the day-to-day planning, monitoring and control of the project. The work of this role is

Figure 12.1

reasonably easy to understand. But very often the Project Manager is not the person providing the funds. The bigger the project, the more likely it is that the Project Manager will have to go to a higher level of management for decisions and commitments on money, the specification of what is needed, the resources required to do the job and acceptance of products developed by the project.

LAYER TWO

This thinking takes us to level two in the diagram, a layer called the Project Board. This consists of those roles that are needed to take those decisions that are too big for the Project Manager's authority level. Examples of questions this Board would answer are:

- Does the Project Manager fully understand what we are looking for?

- Does this look a good way of spending our money?

- Is the proposed solution in line with company strategy?

- The project is not sticking to its planned timeframe and/or budget. Should we continue or close the project?

- Do we want to pay for this major change request?

- Are we prepared to accept the product being offered by the Project Manager?

- Does it meet our requirements?

LAYER ONE

A project may be part of a much larger programme or it may be a major investment for a corporation, a key part of that company's strategy. What I am saying is that a project may be of concern to the very top level of management in the corporation. This would be the top layer in the diagram. This layer is concerned with the business strategy and provides a vision of what the company should look like and what it should be doing in the future. It has to coordinate all the projects going on to change the company to the vision that they have for it. There will come a point when this layer says, 'Hang on, we haven't enough time to handle all the detail, we need to delegate.' So for each project they appoint a Project Board to act on their behalf within certain constraints. These constraints will be addressed in Chapter 14.

LAYER FOUR

There are two simple examples of projects that might need layer four. One is where the skill sets needed are so varied and/or the numbers of resources are so large that no one person has the ability or time to manage the whole thing. Geography may be a factor in deciding whether you need Team Managers. If the developers are in groups some distance away from each other, it is very difficult to manage them all personally.

The other case is where the solution is to be provided by a third party. The external supplier will want to manage its own resources.

Overview

To fulfil the philosophy described at the start of this chapter, I offer for your consideration the PRINCE2 project management team structure (Figure 12.2).

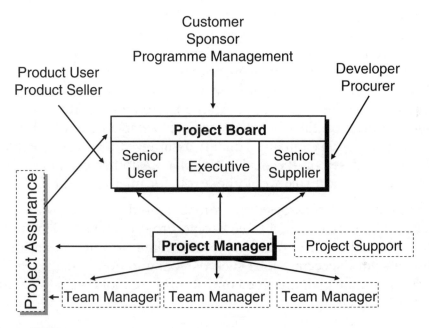

Figure 12.2

The structure allows for the **possible** inclusion of the four layers of management. Whether they are all needed depends on the specific project.

It would be good if we could create a generic project management structure that could be tailored to any project. Without knowing anything about a project's size or complexity we could understand the same organisational terms and by fitting names to these understand quickly who does what. But if we were to have one structure for all sizes of project, it would be important that we made it flexible, a structure that would be adequate for large as well as small projects. The only way in which we can do this is to talk about **roles** that need to be filled, rather than jobs that need to be allocated on a one-to-one basis to individuals. In order to be flexible and meet the needs of different environments and different project sizes, our structure will define roles that might be allocated to one person, shared with others or combined according to a project's needs. Examples are given later in the chapter.

Corporate or programme management hand the decision making for a project to the Project Board. The Project Board members are busy in their own right and haven't the time to look after the project on a day-to-day basis. They delegate this to the Project Managers, reserving for themselves the key stop/go decisions. If they are too busy or do not have the current expertise, they can appoint someone to a Project Assurance role to monitor an aspect of the project on their behalf. A typical example here would be the participation of a company's quality assurance function on behalf of the Senior User or the Senior Supplier. Another example of the Project Assurance role would be a role for internal audit.

Depending on the project environment or the Project Manager's expertise, he or she might need some Project Support. This might be purely administration, such jobs as filing or note taking, but it also includes specialist jobs such as configuration management or expertise in the planning and control software tool that is to be used on the project.

Links

CONTROLS

There are many links between the roles in the project management structure and the controls they exercise. The following are more fully described in Chapter 14.

Layer 1 – Corporate/Programme Management

Corporate/programme management controls the Project Board. They exercise control in a number of ways.

They are responsible for the original terms of reference for the Project Board and therefore control the statement of what the project is to deliver, the scope and any constraints.

They can define the overall targets of the project in terms of delivery dates and budget.

They provide the Project Board with the limits of cash and time at a project level beyond which the Project Board must return to them for a decision on what to do.

They appoint the Executive (very often a member of corporate/programme management) to head the Project Board. They have the power to appoint other members of the Project Board, if they wish to do so.

They indicate what reports at what frequency they want from the Project Board.

Layer 3 – The Project Board

The Project Board has to approve that the project contract (PID) drawn up by the Project Manager is in line with the terms of reference handed down to them (Project Mandate).

Within the project limits set by corporate/programme management the Project Board sets limits of time and budget deviation for each stage of the project. The Project Manager cannot go beyond those limits without fresh authority from the Project Board.

The Project Board has to approve the products of one stage before the Project Manager can move into the next stage.

The Project Board has to approve any change to the original specification. This is more fully discussed in Chapter 17.

A project cannot close without the Project Board confirming that it is prepared to accept the results.

The Project Board stipulates what reports it wants from the Project Manager, their content and frequency.

The Project Board can appoint people to an independent Project Assurance role to monitor various aspects on its behalf.

Layer 3 – The Project Manager

The Project Manager agrees all work with Team Managers (or if that role is not used, with the individual team members).

The Project Manager can set deviation limits for a team's work beyond which it cannot go without the Project Manager's approval. These limits are set within those handed down by the Project Board for the stage.

The Project Manager receives a regular report on each team's progress.

The Project Manager can monitor the quality of work being produced by reference to the quality file, which has to be updated by the Team Managers.

The Project Manager is responsible for the Project and Stage Plans and monitors progress against these.

Layer 4 – The Team Manager

The Team Manager plans the team's work and agrees it with the Project Manager.

The Team Manager holds regular checkpoint meetings with the team.

PLANS

The Project Manager creates and maintains the Project and Stage Plans.

If there is a need for an Exception Plan, the Project Manager creates this.

Team Managers create Team Plans where required.

RISK

The Project Manager maintains a Risk Log.

The Project Board and corporate/programme management are responsible for the identification of risks external to the project.

The Project Manager is responsible for the identification of internal risks.

An owner is appointed from the project management team to keep an eye on each risk.

QUALITY

The Executive is responsible for the quality of the Business Case, at the outset and as the project progresses.

The Senior User role is responsible for the quality of the original specification, for any user acceptance testing, and for confirming that the solution's design and development continue to meet the user needs.

The Senior Supplier role is responsible for the quality of the developed products.

A company's independent quality assurance function may be represented on a project as part of the Project Assurance group.

ACTIVITIES

Filing

A copy of the signed job descriptions for every member of the project management team should be kept in the project file, together with an organisation chart of the structure.

Do's and Don'ts

Don't just use the generic structure slavishly. Use common sense and tailor it, when necessary, to the project.

Don't drop responsibilities. Do move them to another role if that makes more sense for the project in hand.

Do make sure that all responsibilities are given to an appropriate role.

If it's a Large Project

The larger the project the more likely it is that the project organisation structure will need a person to fill each role. In fact the role of Senior User may have to be shared between two or three people in order to get a representative view of the user needs. It would be sensible to control the number of people filling this role. I have seen projects with 15 people clamouring to have a share of this role. The phrase that always comes to mind at such times is 'It will take us half an hour to get the coffee order.' If you are faced with lots of 'volunteers' for the role, organise them into a user committee, which meets and appoints a spokesperson to represent them all. The user committee can instruct the spokesperson on what to ask for, then get feedback from the spokesperson after any Project Board meetings.

Similarly a large project might have lots of suppliers. I do not recommend large numbers of them to share the Senior Supplier role. Two or three might be workable as a maximum, but it shouldn't be allowed to get out of hand. If there are lots of external suppliers, organise the contracts so that there is a main supplier who is responsible for the minor suppliers. Another possibility here is to appoint the company's procurement manager to the role and make that person accountable for obtaining the supplier resources. Before walking away from these ideas on how to restrict the numbers taking these two roles, let me emphasise that a key part of each role is their accountability for quality. The Senior User role is accountable for the quality of the specification. The Senior Supplier role is accountable for the quality of the products supplied as part of the solution. Make sure that you have someone in the roles who picks up this accountability.

There will normally be only one person as Executive. Remember the Executive is the key decision maker. The other roles advise and support the Executive. The Executive is always the person in charge of the purse strings. There may occasionally be projects where the supplier puts up some of the development cash. In such circumstances the supplier would quite correctly take a share of the Executive role.

The division and balance of the decision making would need to be carefully thought out in such cases.

Large projects are more likely to need to appoint people to the Team Manager role. This may be because the project is using external contractors, has people working in different geographical areas or is using a mix of skills beyond the Project Manager's scope.

If it's a Small Project

Let's take an example. Your boss wants you to organise the department's Christmas lunch at one of six restaurants in town for, say, 100 people. Common sense says you don't want a huge number of people in the project management structure. Your boss is paying, so he or she is the Executive. The boss is also defining, or at least approving, the arrangements, and so will also take the Senior User role. In terms of supplier the major resource used is going to be you. Who can commit your time? Right, the boss again, so your Project Board consists of your boss. In terms of Project Assurance, no doubt your boss is capable of checking that personally, so no extra people needed there. You will probably do most, if not all, of the work yourself, so no call for Team Managers. You might get someone to write to the restaurants or ask the staff what their choice of menu is, but that would be the extent of the 'team' that you would need. The remaining question is whether you need any Project Support and in a small project such as this, the answer is likely to be 'No'. So although we began by considering the full project organisation structure, we end up with a structure that looks like Figure 12.3.

All responsibilities are covered without unnecessary numbers of people being involved in their management.

There are two important things to remember:

- Use your common sense. Remember that roles can be combined and ask yourself the question 'OK, who can make that commitment on behalf of the project?'

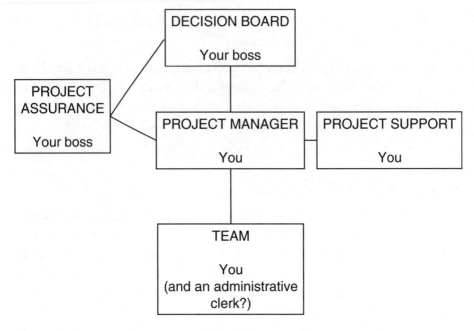

Figure 12.3

- However small the project may be, you can't drop any of the roles or their responsibility and accountability. All you can do is move these to another role.

<table>
<tr><td>

13

</td><td>

Plans

</td></tr>
</table>

Philosophy

A plan is the backbone of every project and is essential for a successful outcome. Good plans cover all aspects of the project, giving everyone involved a common understanding of the work ahead. My friends at Xansa use the following picture (Figure 13.1) to provide a formal definition of a plan.

'A plan is a document, framed in accordance with a pre-defined scheme or method, describing how, when and by whom a specific target or set of targets is to be achieved.'
(PRINCE2)

Figure 13.1

A plan defines:

- The products to be developed or obtained in order to achieve a specified target

- The steps required in order to produce those products
- The sequence of those steps
- Any interdependencies between the products or steps
- How long each step is estimated to take
- When the steps take place
- Who will carry out the steps
- Where controls are to be applied.

A plan:

- Shows in advance whether the target is likely to be achievable
- Shows what resources are needed to accomplish the work
- Shows how long the work will take
- Shows who is to do what and when
- Provides a basis for assessing the risks involved in the work
- Provides the base against which progress can be measured
- Provides the information on the Project Manager's intentions to be communicated to those concerned
- Can be used to gain the consent and commitment of those who have to contribute in some way.

A plan is, however, only a statement of intent. Because something is in our plan does not necessarily mean that it is cast in concrete. There will always be uncertainties.

It is commonly accepted that one of the most common causes of projects failing to deliver benefit is a neglect of the planning process.

There are many reasons advanced for this, one of the most common being that there is 'no time to plan'. What is really being said is that there is a strong desire to start the 'real' work, especially if there is a deadline to be met. The other side of this is where senior management does not recognise the importance of planning, and will not make the necessary time available.

The next excuse given for failure to plan is that there is 'no need'. This is perhaps where:

- The job has been done before
- The project is expected to take only a short time
- The Project Manager prefers to keep all the details 'in the head'.

There are, of course, dangers in these 'reasons' for not planning. Projects are always different, with different people, size, complexity and environments. Short projects can become very long when you realise that you have forgotten something vital. The human brain can retain only a very small number of linked events over a period of several days. When you start adding the details of what is actually happening to what you had planned, it doesn't take long for a required event to get lost somewhere in the brain cells. Project Managers who say that they keep all the details in their head are simply 'fire-fighters'. They lurch from one crisis to the next, always having to put fires out. Sometimes they are hailed as whizz kids because they solve (or waste everybody's time working around) a problem. Most of the problems that they go around solving would not have been there if they had planned properly in the first place! Undertaking a project without planning is just leaving things to chance.

Often people are expected to plan a project with no knowledge of how to go about it. Sadly it is often the case that people are promoted into project management (hence planning) positions without being given the necessary education and training to allow them to do the job effectively. Planning needs to be learned. It is not an inherent skill with which people are born. There are specific techniques (Critical Path Analysis, resource levelling, use of a planning tool, etc.) that need to be learned. Without expertise in these areas, planners are unlikely to do a good job.

The last excuse is that planning is **no fun**! What this means is that planning is hard work. There is a great desire to 'get going' with the stimulating business of the technical challenge.

Overview

This chapter looks at the question of planning for a project.

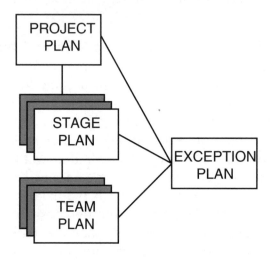

Figure 13.2

HIERARCHY OF PLANS

Figure 13.2 introduces a suggested hierarchy of plans.

At the outset of a project, it is always difficult to plan in detail the activities and resource requirements for the production of all the products required. How accurately can you plan your own activities that you will be doing six months from now? Three months from now? Why should we think it would be an easy task to plan the work for one or more teams of people for the next year (or however long the project may take)? It is nevertheless necessary to provide overall estimates for the project in terms of duration and cost so that approval to proceed can be gained.

Differing levels of management within the project require different levels of detailed plan in order to discharge their responsibility. For instance the Project Board and Project Manager need to assess the continuing viability of the project and therefore require a plan of the total project in overview.

The Project Manager needs to apply control on a day-to-day basis and therefore requires a detailed plan with activities broken down to a small handful of days covering the next period of, say, a few weeks. This is acceptable as long as there is a longer-term view available in less detail – i.e. the Project Plan.

Similarly, if our project uses several teams, the Team Manager will need a detailed plan for the work of the team members. Again it would be sensible to limit this to a short period of time.

We also need to create a new plan, and get it approved by the Project Board, if the original plan goes wrong.

These will now be examined in more detail.

Detail

PROJECT PLAN

The highest level is the Project Plan, which is created at the start of the project. The initial Project Plan is a part of the Project Initiation Document. The Project Plan is a mandatory plan in PRINCE2.

The Project Board does not want to know about every detailed activity in the project. It requires a high level view. This allows the Project Board to know:

- How long the project will take
- What the major deliverables or products will be
- Roughly when these will be delivered
- What people and other resources will have to be committed in order to meet the plan
- How control will be exerted

- How quality will be maintained
- What risks are there in the approach taken.

The Project Board will control the project using the Project Plan as a yardstick of progress.

It is worth remembering the Business Case at this point. The Business Case details (amongst other things) the costs of development and operation of the completed product. The predicted development costs are taken from the Project Plan. These plans are therefore essential to the decision as to whether the proposed system is a viable proposition in business terms.

STAGE PLAN

Having specified the stages and major products in the Project Plan, each stage is then planned in greater detail. This is done, as I just said, just before the end of the previous stage (Figure 13.3).

Stage Plans are mandatory. Unless a project is very small it will be easier to plan in detail one stage at a time. Another part of the philosophy that makes stage planning easier is that a stage is

Stage Plan

- Created at end of previous stage
- Single stage
- More detailed than Project Plan
- Expands project level products
- Narrative and graphical summaries
- Used by Project Manager
- Regular progress monitoring

Figure 13.3

planned shortly before it is due to start, so you have the latest information on actual progress so far available to you.

The procedure at stage planning time involves taking those major products in the Project Plan that are to be created during that stage, and breaking these down (typically) a further two or three levels of detail.

Given that each stage is planned at the end of the preceding one, the planner should now have a clearer view of:

- what has to be produced

- how well the people perform

- how accurate previous estimating has been

than would have been the case earlier in the project.

Stage Plans have the same format as Project Plans.

The Project Manager uses the Stage Plans to track progress on a daily basis through regular progress monitoring.

Plan narrative

The Project and Stage Plans should have a narrative section. Suggested headings for the narrative are as follows:

- Plan description

- Project (and stage) identification

- The plan level, e.g. project or stage

- Summary of the plan and its background

- Intended implementation approach

- How do you intend to implement the plan? Is there anything in the Gantt chart that might need explaining? Some examples might be:

  - You are not starting work on product X as soon as you could because you are waiting for the release of staff from another project

- The construction work looks shorter than normal because we are taking current product Y and modifying it

- The testing work looks longer than normal because we will be testing the product in a hazardous environment.

- Constraints or objectives that have affected the plan

- Quality Plan
The contents of Project and Stage Quality Plans are shown in Appendix 1

- Plan assumptions
On what assumptions is the plan based? Examples are actual staff to be allocated, help or products from other sources at given times. It is essential to list your assumptions. If the Project Board accepts the plan, the Board is accepting your assumptions as reasonable. If your plan goes wrong because an assumption turns out to be incorrect, the Project Board can't throw rocks at you because it agreed with the assumptions. It also gives the Project Board the chance to say if it knows anything about the assumptions that would make them invalid. An example here would be where you create a plan based on the assumption that good old Fred will be your senior technician. If the Senior Supplier knows that he or she has already committed Fred to another project, you can be told and replan. If no one knew of your assumption and you went ahead with the plan, fell behind and came up with the lame excuse, 'I would have been all right if you had given me Fred', noone is going to be too impressed

- Plan prerequisites
Prerequisites are similar to assumptions but they must be in place on day one of the plan in order for the plan to succeed, for example trained staff, equipment and workplace arrangements

- External dependencies
If the plan depends for its success on elements or products that are beyond the Project Manager's control, such as deliv-

eries by suppliers or other projects, these would be identified here

- Risks
  This might be a copy of the entire Risk Log or the Project Board may ask to see only the high probability/high impact risks and the actions you have taken or plan to take

- Tolerance
  What tolerance levels are agreed for the plan?

- Reporting
  The methods, recipients, frequency and formats for reporting during the life of the plan may have been laid down by the Project Board as part of the PID, but may vary according to the duration of a stage. Whatever the case, they should be stated as part of the plan's text.

TEAM PLAN

Team Plans are optional. Their use or otherwise is dictated by the size, complexity and risks associated with the project.

Team Plans are the lowest level of detail and specify activities down to the level of a handful of days, say ten at most. Team Plans may or may not contain the narrative sections associated with the higher levels.

Team Plans will be needed when internal or external teams are to do portions of the work. Part of the Project Manager's job is to cross-relate these plans to the Project and Stage Plans.

EXCEPTION PLAN

Finally, there is the Exception Plan. This is produced when a plan is predicted to exceed the time and cost agreed between the planner and the next higher level of authority. If a Team Plan is forecast to deviate beyond tolerances, the Team Manager must produce the Exception Plan and get approval for its introduction from the Project Manager. If a Stage Plan is forecast to deviate, the Project Manager will produce an Exception Plan and ask the Project Board to allow the Exception Plan to replace the current Stage Plan. If the Project Plan threatens to go beyond its tolerances, the Project Board must take the Exception Plan to corporate or programme management.

The Exception Plan takes over from the plan it is replacing and has the same format.

Links

There is a link between the structure of plans and the controls described in Chapter 14. For example, at an end stage assessment the Project Board will examine the performance of the current Stage Plan and be asked to approve the next Stage Plan. The Team Manager will prepare a Team Plan and agree this with the Project Manager as part of accepting a Work Package.

Do's and Don'ts

By all means use a planning and control tool. It is much easier to modify a plan electronically rather than reach for the eraser. But don't let the tail wag the dog. I have known Project Managers shut themselves in their office for two or three days a week, adjusting the plan to reflect the last set of timesheets. By the time they emerge, things have changed (slightly) again and back they go to tune the plan again. By all means update the plan regularly with actuals. But then stand back and look at what the latest situation is telling you. If you have broken the plan down into sufficient detail, you should be getting warnings of slippage or faster progress than expected. Go out and have a word in the right ears. Can we recover? Can we take advantage of the progress? Is anyone struggling and in need of help? Project progress is often a case of swings and roundabouts. We have a good week followed by a bad week or vice versa. By all means update the plan with actuals every week, but the plan itself should only be modified every two or three weeks on the basis of definite corrective actions we need to take to put the plan back on an even keel. Naturally if an event comes along that we know will require a major change, don't wait. But a lot of small hiccups will sort themselves out if the team knows that you know and have taken an interest in putting things right.

If it's a Large Project

You really will need to use a planning and control tool, a software package. There may already be a standard tool that you are expected to use. Think very carefully about whether you have the time to update it with actuals. In a large project it may well be worth delegating the maintenance of plans to Project Support. Do you have expertise in using the package? Can you afford the time to become an expert?

Many Project Managers struggle to create and update the plans themselves. Many of them have had to learn how to use the tool as they go along. In consequence they know about 10 per cent of the tool's capabilities, and are ignorant of many shortcuts and easier ways of doing things with the plan. The Project Manager's job is to generate the information to build the plan in the first place, use the updated plan as a guide to the status and look ahead for problems or risks.

If it's a Small Project

You may be prepared to put enough detail into the Project Plan to allow you to monitor and control the entire project. If so, no other physically separate plans are needed. But remember that in a small project you need to have broken down the creation of each product to a small handful of days, otherwise you will have insufficient detail against which to monitor progress. Weigh this need for detail against the Project Board's desire to be able to see the entire project on one page.

14 | Controls

Introduction

Project control is perhaps the key element in project management. Some would say that Risk is the cornerstone of project management, but, although I deal with Risk in its own chapter, I see it as one part of control. Whatever your opinion is, I think we can all agree it is vital. I have divided 'control' into the various areas shown in Figure 14.1.

I shall take each one in turn and discuss it under the same headings used for other project management components.

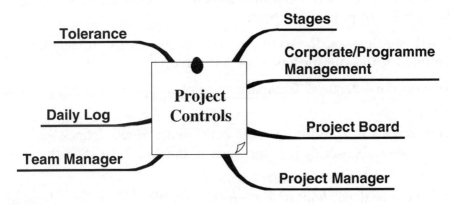

Figure 14.1

PHILOSOPHY

Good control doesn't happen by accident – The control needs of a project need to be assessed and appropriate mechanisms put in place.

Control needs planning – You can't tell whether you are behind or ahead of schedule, above or below budget, unless you have a plan against which you can compare. Setting up project controls is part of the planning process. Failure to plan monitoring and control activities means that they probably won't get done.

Effective monitoring techniques support good control decisions – Without accurate, timely information, project management is blundering about in the dark and constantly reacting to problems rather than preventing or reducing them in advance.

Control needs to be appropriate to the project – As with all other aspects of project management, the level and formality of control should be appropriate for the project.

In setting up any practically-based project control system we will need to put something in place that can, as the project is progressing, answer several fundamental questions.

What was expected to happen? This is where plans are vital. Without them it is not possible to begin!

What *has* happened? Accurate and timely status information is required if this question is to be answered.

What is the difference? Comparison of plans against actuals gives us this.

How serious is it? Without some benchmark which defines 'serious' this cannot be decided. (Tolerance is the key here. See the later explanation.)

What can be done about it? Having got reliable information about all the preceding questions, sensible decisions at the proper level of authority can now be made.

Stages

PHILOSOPHY

The Project Board only gives approval to the Project Manager to proceed one stage at a time. At the end of each stage the Project Board verifies that the project's continuation can still be justified by examining the status of:

- the Business Case

- Risks

- the Project Plan

before it approves a detailed plan to produce the products of the next stage.

A re-examination of the project at the end of each stage allows the Project Board to ask these questions before deciding whether to proceed with the next stage.

Stages give the Project Board these opportunities at formal moments in the project to decide that the project is no longer viable and close it down.

The Project Board wants to be in control without spending all its time on the project. It needs to feel it is making the big decisions, that it will be warned of any major problems in advance, and doesn't want to feel that it has 'a tiger by the tail', in that once started, the project cannot be stopped if it turns sour.

Project Life Cycle and Product Lifespan

A project has a life cycle; the major activities through which it has to pass in order produce the final product. A product has a lifespan, running from the original idea through its development and use, until it is finally withdrawn from use. The two are often confused. Figure 14.2 shows the two together to clarify the differences.

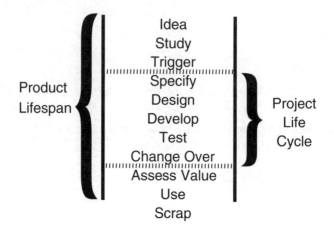

Figure 14.2

Technical Stages

The project life cycle consists of a set of technical stages, each of which is distinguished by the production of one or more specific end products. These products serve as the input for the next stage until we have developed the final products of the project.

MANAGEMENT STAGES

What have been described so far in this chapter are technical stages, those parts of the project identified by their use of different techniques to produce the various technical products. But now consider the division into stages from the view of the Project Board. The Project Board is driven by the need to control and approve the gradual progress of the project, confirming that the Business Case still exists as well as assuring itself that the various products meet the identified needs. This gives a different perspective on the use of stages.

What is a management stage? A management stage is a collection of activities and products whose delivery is managed as a unit. As such, it is a section of the project, and it is the element of work that the Project Manager is managing on behalf of the Project Board at any one time.

WHY PLAN IN STAGES?

How can I make sure I stay in control?

How can I limit the risks?

How can I stop it if it goes wrong?

_____

Too much time planning

Too far ahead

Too many unknowns

Too much guesswork

Figure 14.3

PROJECT BOARD REASONS FOR STAGES

The Project Board wants to be in control without spending all its time on the project. It needs to feel it is making the big decisions, that it will be warned of any major problems in advance, and doesn't want to feel that it has 'a tiger by the tail', in that once started, the project cannot be stopped if it turns sour.

With risky projects there is the need to pause and make sure that the risks are still controllable, so risky projects are likely to have more, smaller stages.

The reasons, therefore, for breaking projects into management stages are to give the Project Board opportunities for conscious decision making as to whether to continue with the project or not, based upon:

- A formal analysis of how the project is performing, based on information about results of the current stage

- An assessment of the next Stage Plan

- A check on what impact the next Stage Plan will have on the overall Project Plan

- A check to confirm that the business justification for the project and product is still valid

- Confirmation that the risks facing the project are manageable.

A re-examination of the project at the end of each stage allows the Project Board to ask these questions before deciding whether to proceed with the next stage.

Stages give the Project Board these opportunities at formal moments in the project to decide that the project is no longer viable and close it down. They key criterion for decision making in business terms is the viability of the Business Case. Is the justification for what we are doing still valid? If not, the project should be in jeopardy. If it is, then it should go forward. These decisions are made in the light of the strategic or programme objectives.

Unless the project is broken into management stages to provide suitable points at which to make the decisions, the Project Board cannot be fully in control of the project and its resources. Figure 14.3 illustrates the benefits of planning in stages from the perspective of both the Project Board and the Project Manager.

PROJECT MANAGER REASONS FOR STAGES

For their part, the Project Manager does not want to spend huge amounts of time at the outset trying to plan a long project in sufficient detail for day-to-day control. Trying to look ahead, say, nine months and plan in detail what will happen and who will do what is almost certain to be wrong. How much easier it is to plan just the next few weeks in detail and have only a high level plan of the whole project.

Stage ends are needed to obtain from the Project Board the required commitment of resources, money and equipment to move into the next stage.

Stage-limited commitment – At the end of each stage the Project Board only approves a detailed plan to produce the products of the next stage. The Project Plan is updated, but this is mainly for the guidance of the Project Board and will become more accurate as more stages are completed.

Sign-off of interim end-products – At the end of each stage, the interim end-products are reviewed by all affected organisational functions, particularly those that will use the end products in order to develop the products of the next stage. Throughout the life cycle, the concept of feedback is important. The end products from any stage must be compared with that of previous stages to ensure that a correct translation has been made. The general trend through the life cycle is towards a progressively more explicit, more detailed, more accurate, and more complete end product.

In theory, at the end of each stage, the Project Board can call for cancellation of the project because of the existence of one or more possibly critical situations. For example, the organisation's business needs may have changed to the point at which the project is no longer cost effective. A project may also be cancelled if the estimated cost to complete the project exceeds the available funds. In practice, however, cancellation of a project becomes progressively more difficult to justify as increasing amounts of resources are invested.

In-stage reviews – As each product of a stage is produced it should be reviewed for completeness and quality. All major product reviews should include representatives from the user community as well as the relevant technical experts. Other reviewers might come, for example, from an independent quality assurance function. As a result, the final end stage assessment by the Project Board is more of a formality because most problems and mistakes have been spotted early on and corrected.

The in-stage reviews can be carried out formally as walkthroughs or inspections or can be informal peer group sessions. How they are carried out depends a great deal upon what is appropriate for the specific project and upon the degree of rigour imposed by the methodology being used.

Generic task lists – No matter how different the systems being developed are and how different the end products for identical stages, there is one generic set of tasks to be carried out, regardless of the methodology chosen. Therefore, if the same methodology is used to develop different systems, this set of generic tasks varies little, if at all, from project to project. Since there is little variation in the set of generic tasks, product consistency is ensured and activities are not omitted, either through oversight or ignorance.

TECHNICAL STAGES VERSUS MANAGEMENT STAGES

There may or may not be an exact match between technical and management stages. For example, in a small project the Project Board may be happy to approve a plan that combines two or more technical stages. On the other hand, if one technical stage will take many months to complete, the Project Board may ask for it to be broken into two or more management stages for the purposes of planning and control.

PROJECT INITIATION STAGE

However large or small the project, it is sensible to begin a project with what is referred to as an initiation stage. This is where the Project Board and Project Manager decide if there is agreement on:

- What the project is to achieve
- Why it is being undertaken
- Who is to be involved and in what role
- How and when the required products will be delivered.

This information is documented in the PID, which is then frozen and used as a benchmark throughout the project, and at the end by the Project Board, to check the focus and progress of the project.

Even in a tiny project with a Project Board of one person it is sensible to begin with an initiation stage. In a small project it may only take half an hour or so to get this understanding, but an amazing number of projects get into trouble because of misunderstandings at the outset. It is very easy to make assumptions on what you think is needed – and get it wrong. If you start the project by heading off in the wrong direction, then you only need to be slightly wrong to waste a lot of time, money and effort. It is also easy for a member of a Project Board to forget the original agreement and begin to think that something quite different was requested. Documenting the initial agreed objectives and scope and who was committed to do what can save the Project Manager from many arguments and headaches later on in the project.

LINKS

The concept of stages links to end stage assessments by the Project Board.

There is also a link to risks. As mentioned before, the riskier the project, the shorter and more frequent the stages may be to enable a formal risk review to be done by the Project Board as part of the decision whether to continue.

Another link is to the tolerance levels, described next in this chapter. It gives the Project Board tighter control to set Exception limits for the next stage than simply to have exception limits for the entire project.

DO'S AND DON'TS

Always have an initiation stage, however short the project.

Don't split a project into more stages than Project Board control requires.

Don't have a stage that is longer than you can comfortably plan in detail. Remember, a Stage Plan is going to be the Project Manager's main basis for control. This means that you need to get each piece of work that you hand out down to a few days. This will allow you to monitor whether the work is slipping or not. A fact of life is that people only realise they will not finish on time when they get near the target date. If the pieces of work are 20 days or more in duration, then by the time the person tells you they will be late, it is usually too late to put any exception actions in place.

IF IT'S A LARGE PROJECT

The stage-limited commitment, which is sometimes referred to as a 'creeping commitment,' is especially important for large projects with a rapidly changing environment that makes it almost impossible to develop an accurate plan for the total project at the outset. However, this type of commitment requires that the provider of funds for the project must accept that the estimate for the completion of the system will inevitably change with time.

IF IT'S A SMALL PROJECT

Even in a tiny project with a Project Board of one person it is sensible to begin with an initiation stage. In a small project it may only take half an hour or so to get this understanding, but an amazing number of projects get into trouble because of misunderstandings at the outset. It is very easy to make assumptions on what you think is needed – and get it wrong. If you start the project by heading off in the wrong direction, then you only need to be slightly wrong to waste a lot of time, money and effort. It is also easy for a member of a Project Board to forget the original agreement and begin to think that something quite different was requested. Documenting the initial agreed objectives and scope and who was committed to do what can save the Project Manager from many arguments and headaches later on in the project.

Tolerance

PHILOSOPHY

- Tolerances are the permissible deviation from a plan without having to refer the matter to the next higher level of authority.

No project has ever gone 100 per cent to plan. There will be good days and bad days, good weeks and bad weeks. If the Project Board is going to 'manage by exception' it doesn't want the Project Manager running to it, saying, 'I've spent a pound more than I should today' or 'I've fallen half a day behind schedule this week.'

But equally the Project Board doesn't want the project to overspend by a £ million or slip two months behind schedule without being warned. So where is the dividing line? What size of deviation from the plan is acceptable without going back to the Board for a decision? These margins are the tolerances.

The second philosophical point about tolerances is that we don't wait for tolerances to be exceeded; we forecast this, so that the next higher level of authority has time to react and possibly prevent or reduce the deviation.

OVERVIEW

The two main elements of tolerance are time and cost. Other elements that may be considered are scope and quality.

If we remember the four levels of project management:

- Corporate/programme management sets the project tolerances within which the Project Board has to remain

- The Project Board agrees stage tolerances with the Project Manager

- The Project Manager agrees tolerances for a Work Package with a Team Manager.

Figure 14.4 will help to explain the concept.

As long as the plan's actual progress is within the tolerance margins, all is well. As soon as it can be **forecast** that progress will deviate outside the tolerance margins, the next higher level of authority needs to be advised.

DETAIL

Project tolerances should be part of the Project Mandate handed down by corporate/programme management. If they are not there, it is the Executive's job to find out from corporate/programme management what they are.

The Project Board sets stage tolerances for the Project Manager within the overall project tolerances that they have received. The

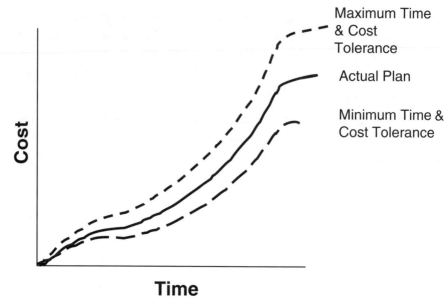

Figure 14.4

portion allocated to a stage should depend on the risk content of the work, the extent of the unknowns (such as technologies never used before, resources of unknown ability, or tasks never attempted before).

The Project Manager negotiates appropriate tolerances for each Work Package with the Team Manager. Again these will be tolerances within the stage tolerances set for the Project Manager.

LINKS

There is a link to the 'Controlling a Stage' process that will bring any forecast deviation to the notice of the appropriate level of authority.

DO'S AND DON'TS

What do we do if a project has such a tight deadline that our shortest plan can only just achieve that date, i.e. we are offered no time tolerance? We try to enlarge the cost tolerance. This would allow us to pay for overtime, extra resources, better equipment, better resources, anything that might save time if the target date was threatened.

If the converse was true and no cost tolerance was offered, we would ask for a greater time tolerance. This would allow us not to use overtime, drop some resources, use cheaper resources.

If both time and cost tolerances are tight, this is where we look at the other two elements, scope and quality. For scope we list everything we have to deliver in order of priority. Then if the going gets tough, we take the list to the customer and say, 'You can't have everything within the tolerances. What products can we drop?'

Quality is the dangerous aspect of tolerance. This is because quality reduction can happen without your knowing. If a team knows that it is under time and/or cost pressure, the easiest thing to do is relax on the quality checking, carry out fewer tests, let things slip through that you know aren't exactly right. Occasionally there may be quality concessions that can be made in order to stay within other tolerances, such as 'You can have all the products, but you can't have the colours you wanted.'

IF IT'S A LARGE PROJECT

It is very important to establish tolerances at all the levels described. The Project Manager should consider carefully any tolerances for scope and quality that may be called upon. Priorities for the various elements of the product need to be agreed at the beginning so that they can influence the sequence of design and development. There would be no point in trying to downscope late in the project if all the minor 'nice-to-have's have already been developed.

IF IT'S A SMALL PROJECT

There will probably be no Team Managers. In that case the Project Manager may still wish to allow a small tolerance for an individual's Work Package. The danger in telling an individual that they have a certain tolerance is that the tolerance becomes the expected target. For example, if you tell a person that they have until Thursday to do a job with a tolerance of one day, in their mind the target becomes Friday. Some managers prefer to set tolerances but keep these to themselves.

Management Controls

Management controls work around the three areas of getting a project off to a controlled start, controlling progress and bringing the project to a controlled close. Let's take a look at the necessary management controls following our concept of up to four levels of management: corporate/programme management, Project Board, Project Manager and Team Manager.

Corporate/Programme Management Controls

PHILOSOPHY

Corporate/programme management will have many things on its mind and will want to spend the minimum of time on any one project while still retaining control. This is the start of 'management by exception'. They agree the overall project objectives, time and cost objectives with the Executive of the Project Board and say 'Get on with it. As long as you are on course, just send us the odd Highlight Report. But come back to us if you forecast that you are moving outside the limits we have agreed with you.'

OVERVIEW

For the maximum amount of confidence in their Project Board, corporate/programme management should normally appoint one of their members to be the Executive. They can appoint people to other Project Board roles or leave the selection to the Executive.

DETAIL

Project Mandate

Corporate/programme management will be responsible for the creation of the Project Mandate, which they will pass to the Executive of the Project Board. This gives them control over the project's objectives, scope and constraints.

Customer's Quality Expectations

As part of the Project Mandate corporate/programme management should specify their quality expectations of the final product. This should cover such things as finish, performance, reliability, and maintainability.

Project Closure

It is a job for the Executive to confirm with corporate/programme management that its Project Mandate has been satisfied by the detail provided by, first, the Project Brief and later the PID.

LINKS

Corporate/programme management set the project tolerances. This allows them to define the circumstances under which the Project Board must refer problems to them for a go/no go decision, rather than make the decision itself.

There will be entries in the Communication Plan to describe how the Project Board, or at least the Executive, will keep corporate/programme management informed.

A higher level architecture group may prescribe the project approach where the project is part of a programme. It will have to conform to the same architecture as the other parts of the programme. The Project Board, especially the Senior Supplier, has to check this.

DO'S AND DON'TS

Do keep reports and meetings to a sensible minimum. Try to avoid the monthly progress meetings where your project is one item on a crowded corporate/programme agenda.

Do avoid appointing the Project Board from below, i.e. without reference to corporate/programme management. This only leads to mistrust of the Project Board by corporate/programme management. If this happens, any so-called 'decision' by the Project Board will ping-pong between them and corporate/programme management for approval by the latter. What you are looking for is a Project Board that has the confidence of corporate/programme management, so that once the Project Board has taken a decision you can move on.

IF IT'S A LARGE PROJECT

The controls and reporting should be documented and copies kept by the Project Manager.

IF IT'S A SMALL PROJECT

It is unlikely that a small project will interest corporate/programme management. In this case the Executive will assume the role.

Project Board Controls

PHILOSOPHY

The Project Board wants to 'manage by exception', i.e. agree a Stage Plan with the Project Manager and then let them get on with it without any interference or extra effort – unless the plan looks like going wrong.

OVERVIEW

The Project Board 'owns' the project. Its members are ultimately accountable for the success of the project, not the Project Manager. This is why the Project Board members must have the requisite authority to commit resources and make decisions.

Project Board members will be busy with their other jobs, and therefore will want to spend the minimum amount of time controlling the project commensurate with making sure that the project meets its objectives within the defined constraints. Like corporate/programme management, it wants to 'manage by exception'.

DETAIL

Controlled Start

Project Mandate/Project Brief The Project Mandate should contain the project objectives, Customer Quality Expectations and Project Approach, among other things. One of the first tasks in PRINCE2 is to add any missing information, turning the Project Mandate into the Project Brief. It is therefore very important for the Project Board to examine this document and be satisfied with its contents before agreeing to initiate the project.

Initiation Stage Plan   The Project Board examines the plan to see if it is appropriate to the work needed to initiate the project. This will be affected by any previous work done if the project is part of an overall programme.

Project Tolerances   Corporate/programme management sets tolerances for the whole project. It is the Executive's job to ensure this information is made available at the outset of a project as part of the Project Mandate.

Project Initiation Document   The Project Initiation Document (PID) is the internal 'contract' for the project, documenting what the project is to do, why it should be done (the Business Case), who is responsible for what, when and how products are to be delivered. There has to be agreement by customer and supplier on its contents before commitment to the project by the Project Board. If a viable Business Case does not exist, the Project Board should not proceed with the project.

Controlled Progress

Stage Tolerances The Project Board defines the maximum deviations allowed from the Stage Plan without the Project Manager having to return to the Board for a decision on action to be taken. This is the key element of 'management by exception'.

Highlight Reports   The best way of characterising **management by exception** is the expression 'no news is good news'. At a frequency defined by the Project Board in the Project Initiation Document, the Project Manager has to send a Highlight Report to the Project Board to confirm achievements towards meeting the Stage Plan.

The frequency of Highlight Reports is determined by the Project Board during initiation, but is typically produced monthly.

The Project Manager prepares Highlight Reports, using progress information provided by the team members and analysed at the checkpoints.

The principal focus of the Highlight Report is to identify:

- Products completed during the current reporting period

- Products to be completed in the next period

- Any real or potential problems.

Other limited narrative information, such as the budget and risk status, can be added – up to a total of one page of paper.

Change Request Approval   Having approved the objectives and products required in the project initiation, it is only right that the Project Board should have to approve any changes to them. Once requested changes have been estimated for the effort and cost of doing them, the customer has to decide on their priority, whether they should be done and whether the money to do them can be found. As for all the other decisions, it needs an assessment of the impact on the Project Plan, the Business Case and the risk situation.

Exception Reports   If the Project Manager can forecast that the plan will end outside its tolerance margins, an Exception Report must be sent immediately to the Project Board, detailing the problem, options and a recommendation.

It should be stressed that if the project is not collecting reliable progress information, it will be difficult to know when that point has been reached.

Exception Plan   If the Project Board, on reading the Exception Report, decides to accept a recommendation to proceed on the basis of a modified plan, it will ask the Project Manager to produce an Exception Plan, which replaces the remainder of the plan.

The technical term for exceeding (or predicting that you will exceed) tolerance is 'exception'. When the project is facing an Exception, the formal approach dictates that the Project Manager should prepare an Exception Plan and present it to the Project Board for approval. The less formal approach says that there may not be a meeting, but the Project Manager still needs to get his/her plan of remedial action approved by the Project Board.

End Stage Assessment   The end stage assessment happens – surprise, surprise – at the end of each management stage, where the Project Board assesses the continued viability of the project and, if satisfied, gives the Project Manager approval to proceed with the next stage.

The Project Board must be aware of the need to avoid technical or irrelevant discussions and to focus on the management aspects which, when taken as a whole, inform its decision on whether to proceed or not. As a rule of thumb an end stage assessment should not last more than two hours, even for a large project. A sensible Project Manager will have been in touch with the Project Board, either verbally or in Highlight Reports, making sure that the members know what is coming and finding out what they think about the future of the project. 'No surprises' is the best way to ensure short end stage assessments.

Of course, the 'bottom line' is whether the project is still predicted to deliver sufficient benefits to justify the investment, i.e. is the Business Case still sound?

The other aspects of the end stage assessment are:

- Current progress checked against Project Plans
- Current stage completed successfully (all products delivered and accepted)

- Next Stage Plan examined and authorised

- Confirmation that all delivered stage products have passed their predefined quality checks

- Approval to proceed form signed by all Project Board members.

The Project Board must sign the approval to proceed form, so that the project cannot drift without approval into the next stage.

Next Stage Plan   At the same time as the End Stage Report is given, the Project Manager presents the next Stage Plan to the Project Board. This should be compared against the Project Plan. The next stage cannot proceed until the Project Board approves its Stage Plan.

The detail of the next Stage Plan may often cause modification of the Project Plan. The Project Board checks the figures against both the previous version of the Project Plan and the revised version to see what changes have been made. Any changes should be justified (e.g. against approved requests for change) before approval of the Stage Plan.

Controlled Close

End Project Report   As part of its decision on whether the project may close the Project Board receives an End Project Report from the Project Manager, summing up the project's performance in meeting the requirements of the Project Initiation Document plus any changes that were made. It is similar to an End Stage Report, but covers the entire project.

Any changes that were made after the Project Initiation Document was agreed are identified, and their impact on Project Plan, Business Case and risks is assessed.

The report provides statistics on Project Issues and their impact on the project, plus statistics on the quality of work carried out. It is created by the Project Manager and submitted to the Project Board.

Project Initiation Document   The Project Board uses the original Project Initiation Document to confirm that the project has achieved its original objectives, including the required quality.

Issue Log   This is used together with the Project Initiation Document to check how the original objectives of the project were modified. It is also used to match against the Follow-on Action Recommendations to ensure that there are no loose ends.

Quality File   The Quality File gives the Project Board an assessment of whether the appropriate quality work was put into the project's products and whether there is an audit trail available.

Follow-on   Action   Recommendations   The   Follow-on   Action Recommendations document any unfinished business at the end of the project.

For example, there may have been a number of requests for change that the Project Board decided not to implement during the project, but which were not rejected. Not all expected products may have been handed over, or there may be some known problems with what has been delivered.

The Follow-on Action Recommendations allow the Project Board to direct any unfinished business to the person or group whose job it will be to have the recommendations considered for action after the current project has ended.

The Project Board is presented with a list of all outstanding actions that are to be handed to the group that will support the product in its operational life. These may be change requests that the Project Board decided not to implement during the life of the current project or risks identified during the project that may affect the product in use. The Project Board has to confirm that all outstanding issues have been captured, and satisfy itself that nothing on the list should have been completed by the project.

Post-Project Review Plan   Normally many products need time in use before the achievement of their expected benefits can be measured. This measurement after a period of use is an activity called a

Post-Project Review. The Executive on the Project Board will be responsible for ensuring that these measurements take place. The Project Manager has to provide a plan for how, when and by whom these measurements are to be done.

The Post-Project Review occurs outside the project and, as such, is not part of the project.

Any corrective work identified by the Post-Project Review would be done during product use and maintenance. Any problems may not be with the product itself, but organisational ones, needing such solutions as retraining.

The Post-Project Review can happen perhaps 6, 12 or 18 months after the project has finished (it depends on the nature of the product).

Lessons Learned Report The Project Manager has to present a report on what project management (and possibly technical) aspects of the project went well, and what went badly. The Project Board has the job of ensuring that this is passed to an appropriate body that will disseminate the report to other projects and possibly modify the relevant standards. It is important that an appropriate group is identified. There may be a project management support group or a quality assurance group.

Customer Acceptance The Project Manager should seek confirmation of customer acceptance of the end product(s) before asking the Project Board to allow the project to close.

LINKS

There is a link to the setting of tolerances, particularly stage tolerances.

Another link is to the change control mechanism, because the Project Board makes the decision on whether changes are to be implemented or not.

Do's and don'ts

Do make sure that you get sign-off from the Project Board, confirming that the project **as defined in the Project Initiation Document** has been completed and the end product accepted. However small the project has been, never assume that the end product has been accepted.

Don't allow the Project Board to let the project drift on into modifying the end product or creating extra products outside the scope of what was agreed during initiation. Any such work thought up by the customer when you deliver what you believe to be the end product should form part of another project and another Project Initiation Document. You will not be able to measure the success of the project fairly if you allow time and cost to be added for work that is not covered in the Project Initiation Document. Remember, project success is measured against the Project Initiation Document **plus any approved change requests**. It is your own Business Case that will suffer if you allow last minute 'wouldn't it be nice if' tinkering to creep in.

If it's a large project

All of these controls should be used and documented.

If it's a small project

Many of these controls can be done informally, but the Project Board should always consider what documentation of its decisions is needed in case things turn sour later.

Project Manager Controls

Philosophy

A project is broken down into stages. The Project Manager is in day-to-day control of a stage based on a Stage Plan that the Project Board has approved. The Project Manager carries on with a stage until its end without needing another approval from the Project Board unless either:

- There is a forecast of an exception beyond tolerance limits; or

- Changes have been requested for which extra resources are needed.

OVERVIEW

The basic idea is to:

- Agree with the Project Board what is to be done and the constraints within which the job has to be done

- Get approval from the Project Board for a plan to do the work

- Direct teams or individuals to do the necessary work

- Confirm with the customer that the products meet requirements

- Report back that the job has been done.

Breaking a project into stages, using tolerance levels and agreeing the need for any Highlight Reports with the Project Board complement this basic concept.

DETAIL

Controlled Start

Starting up a Project (SU) This is a pre-project process, which allows the Project Manager to gather enough information about the objectives of the project in order to prepare a plan for the Initiation stage.

Initiating a Project (IP) This process allows the Project Manager to collect together all the information about the work to be done plus the justification for the project, and get it agreed by the Project Board.

Customer's Quality Expectations The Project Manager must ensure that the expectations have been defined before the initiation stage. This is the start point for quality in the project. If they are missing, it is the customer's job to obtain them.

Project Approach The Project Approach defines the method of providing the solution to the project's needs. Examples of a Project Approach are:

- Do we do it ourselves from scratch?
- Do we modify an existing product to make the new product?
- Do we ask another company to make it for us?
- Can we buy a ready-made product?

The Project Approach may have already been defined if the project is part of a programme, e.g. 'We have already decided that we are going to use IBM mainframes for our banking computing, so please don't suggest a design for your part of the programme that uses Hewlett Packard equipment.' The Project Manager has to decide whether the Project Approach to be provided has already been defined prior to the project, or whether it is part of the job at this time to say what that solution will be.

Project Brief The Project Manager adds any missing information about the project's objectives to the Project Mandate.

Project Plan The Project Plan is a high level view of the whole project created at the outset as part of the information required by the Project Board on whether to commit to the project.

Acceptance Criteria Acceptance criteria should be agreed with the Senior User at the outset. This list defines a checklist of criteria. If at the end of the project it is agreed that all criteria have been met, then the Project Manager can ask for closure of the project as having met its targets.

Controlled Progress

Quality File   The Project Manager enters details of all planned quality work in the file. Those responsible for carrying out the quality work update it with actual results. The Project Manager then monitors this on a regular basis.

Work Packages   A Work Package is an agreement between the Project Manager and either an individual or a Team Manager to undertake a piece of work. It describes the work, agreed dates, standards to be used, quality and reporting requirements. No work can start without the Project Manager's approval via a Work Package, so it is a powerful schedule, cost and quality control for the Project Manager.

Team Plans   Where the Project Manager is dealing with several teams, as part of agreement on a Work Package, the Project Manager has to agree the team plan to produce the products involved. This is then reflected in the Stage Plan. The Project Manager can use this to confirm that the plan is reasonable, will fit within the stage tolerances given by the Project Board, and that it contains adequate quality work.

Checkpoint Reports   This is a Highlight Report from a team to the Project Manager. It is sent at a frequency agreed in the Work Package.

A specific aim of a checkpoint report is to check all aspects of the Work Package against the team and Stage Plans to ensure that there are no nasty surprises. Useful questions to answer are: 'What is not going to plan?' and 'What is likely not to go to plan?' The crucial question that underlies the objective of the meeting is 'Are we still likely to complete the stage within the tolerances laid down by the Project Manager?'

Checkpoints should be taken as frequently as the Project Manager requires. They may coincide with the Project Manager's need to consider replanning. Overall, the checkpoint frequency is determined at project initiation and stage planning time, but usually occurs weekly.

The information gathered at a checkpoint is recorded for the Project Manager and forms the basis of the Highlight Report.

Issue Log   The Issue Log is a key control document for the Project Manager, keeping track of all problems and change requests. It usually contains the answer to Project Board questions such as 'Why is the project going to cost more/take longer than you said in the project initiation?'

Quality File   The Project Manager monitors this to check that quality inspections are taking place as planned, and also to check for quality problems.

Risk Log   The status of risks should be monitored regularly. They are formally reviewed at each stage end, but should also be checked as part of the impact analysis of major change requests.

Activity Network   The activity network shows what is on the critical path at the moment and how much float an activity has. This is useful to the Project Manager in knowing what to check on, which delays are serious and which are not.

Stage Plan   The Stage Plan is the document against which the Project Manager is controlling.

Configuration Management   Configuration management is the identification of the products to be created/used by the project, their tracking and control. This provides the Project Manager with the status of products.

Daily Log

PHILOSOPHY

Apart from the Stage Plan a Project Manager often needs a diary to record significant events or remind him or herself of little jobs to do in the coming week.

OVERVIEW

The Project Manager keeps a Daily Log in which to record important events, decisions, happenings or statements. This is partly a defence mechanism in case some time later the other person forgets that they said something, but also to become part of the Project Manager's monitoring that what was said actually happens.

It is also useful for the Project Manager to set up a number of monitoring activities for the coming week.

DETAIL

Before the start of each week the Project Manager should take a look at the Stage Plan, the Risk Log, the Issue Log and the Quality File. This should provide a number of monitoring points for action during the week, such as:

- What is on the critical path of my plan that is supposed to finish during the week? Is it going to finish on time? (Or else?) Did it finish on time?

- Should the status of any risks be checked this week? Is it time to give a risk owner a nudge to follow up on the risk's status?

- Are there any outstanding Project Issues that I should be chasing which are out for impact analysis or for consideration by the customer?

Controlled Close

Acceptance Criteria   If all acceptance criteria can be ticked, this puts the Project Manager in a strong position to say that the project has achieved its objectives and can close.

Configuration Management   The Configuration Librarian does a check on all products produced and their status. This confirms that all products have been approved, a necessary check before work to close the project can begin. This area will also be responsible for delivering the end product to the operational support group.

Issue Log   All Project Issues should have either been dealt with or have Project Board agreement to being held over and passed to the operational support group. The Project Manager must check the status of all issues as part of closing the project.

Customer Acceptance   The Project Manager must obtain some form of customer acceptance before the Project Board can be asked to confirm project closure. Depending on the project, this may be formal or informal.

Operation and Maintenance Acceptance   The group who will take over responsibility for the end product in its operational life must agree that they are prepared to do so, i.e. that the product is in an acceptable state.

LINKS

Controls link to Chapter 12 as part of the 'who does what'.

There is a link to the work needed in 'Starting Up a Project' (SU).

There are links to Change Control and Configuration Management.

There is a link to the Project Manager's Daily Log.

DO'S AND DON'TS

Do check the need for all these points against the environment of the project.

Do not be misled by the comfortable feeling at the start of a project that everybody is committed, and behind you. This is the direction from which back-stabbing occurs! That 'togetherness' feeling can evaporate as problems and/or changes come along. I used to work for a very cynical Italian manager whose favourite phrase was, 'Don't plan for the honeymoon, plan for the divorce.' In other words, if everything in the project was to go sweetly, the 'honeymoon' feeling would last and there would be little need for controls and documentation of who agreed to do what and why. But life has a way of changing, people change their minds, forget things, unexpected events occur. Just in case things turn sour you need to have the controls mentioned in this chapter available to you and to be able to lay your hands on documentation to support why the project did what it did.

IF IT'S A LARGE PROJECT

All of these items should be considered for use. Their documentation and safe filing should also be considered as they will form a key part of the Project Manager's audit trail of why things happened and who decided what.

IF IT'S A SMALL PROJECT

Many of the controls can be done informally. There may be no teams or only the one reporting direct to the Project Manager with no Team Managers appointed. This shortens the checkpoint control. The Project Manager would hold the checkpoint meetings with the team and write up the Checkpoint Report personally.

Team Manager Controls

PHILOSOPHY

The Team Manager may work for an external supplier. Even when the Team Manager works for the same organisation as the Project Manager, they may have different line managers. Therefore there has to be a means of agreeing work to be done, reporting progress and returning the completed work.

OVERVIEW

The controls between Project Manager and Team Manager, Team Manager and team member are based around the Work Package.

DETAIL

Work Packages   A Work Package is an agreement between the Project Manager and a Team Manager to undertake a piece of work. It describes the products to be delivered, agreed dates, standards to be used, quality, reporting and approval requirements. The Team Manager has to ensure that the requirements of a Work Package are realistic before accepting it on behalf of the team. If agreement cannot be reached with the Project Manager, the matter would be referred to the Project Board.

Team Plans   As part of agreement on a Work Package, the Team Manager has to prepare the Team Plan to produce the involved products. The Project Manager should agree tolerances for the work that are within the stage tolerances.

Quality Log   The Project Manager enters details of all planned quality checks for the Work Package in the log. The Team Manager has to ensure that it is updated with actual results from the team's work.

Checkpoints   A checkpoint is a time-driven, team level control mechanism, where the status of work in a stage or of a team is ascertained. It may or may not be a formal meeting.

It involves the people carrying out the work and is triggered by the Team Manager. In larger projects the participants might be the Project Manager, Team Manager and Project Assurance people. In smaller projects it might be just the Team Manager and the team members themselves.

A specific aim of a checkpoint is to check all aspects of the team-work against the plans to ensure that there are no nasty surprises. Useful questions are: 'What have we delivered?' and 'What is not going according to plan?' The crucial question that underlies the objective of the meeting is 'Are we still likely to complete the work within the tolerances laid down by the Project Manager?'

A checkpoint can also be used for the downward dissemination of information from the Project Board and corporate/programme management by having them attend occasionally and talk to team members.

Checkpoints should be taken as frequently as the Project Manager requires in order to maintain control over progress. They may coincide with the Project Manager's need to consider replanning. Overall, the checkpoint's frequency is determined at project initiation and stage planning time, but usually occurs weekly.

Timesheets In support of Checkpoint Reports, the Project Manager may ask for timesheets, giving information on product start and completion dates or revised dates. This is used to update the Stage Plan.

Timesheets are the standard method of recording time spent on project work and are a prime source of project progress data capture.

They are generally familiar to most people and their use is understood. However, a few points need to be remembered if their use as a monitoring device is to be effective.

In order to gain a clear picture of all time (and hence costs) spent on the project, it is important that everybody involved fills in timesheets.

One of the historical problems with timesheets is that they tend to be inaccurate. Accurate monitoring information is a prerequisite to sensible control decisions.

Timesheets also need to be returned regularly and promptly. The later monitoring information is received, the later vital control decisions will be made.

Timesheets should also be capable of being accurately filled in. Often, people do not do this because there are, for instance, no codes for particular types of work or products.

The above point is reinforced by the concept that timesheets should allow for non-project work to be entered.

How often should timesheets be collected? The answer is (of course) as often as the Project Board has specified in the Project and Stage Plans. The typical interval is one week. Clearly, once the effort expended has been recorded, then the cost of production can be derived.

Very often too much data is collected on timesheets. The more you ask for, the less likely the figures will be accurate. On a Friday afternoon I have often seen people staring at the ceiling, musing 'Now what was I doing on Monday?' If you do want to track genuine effort used, I believe that the Project Manager should spot check daily completion of the timesheet. But unless there is a genuine need to collect actual effort as part of improving estimating ability, I think that timesheet information can be reduced to three questions:

- When did I start this product?

- Is it finished?

- If not, do I need to revise the end date?

LINKS

There is a link to quality. Another link is to Chapter 13.

The Product Delivery process includes detail of the Team Manager's work and should be read in conjunction with this section of the chapter.

DO'S AND DON'TS

Do read the 'Managing Product Delivery' (MP) process.

Do think about the environment of the project, the political situation, and the relationship between customer and supplier.

Do tune the needs of Team Manager control to the environment.

IF IT'S A LARGE PROJECT

The Team Manager may work for different management to that of the Project Manager. This presents the problem of different objectives, a different Business Case to which the Team Manager must work. To avoid being caught in the squeeze between customer and supplier, or between one supplier and another, the Team Manager should follow the guidelines in the 'Managing Product Delivery' (MP) process.

IF IT'S A SMALL PROJECT

There will probably not be more than one team, and therefore this section will be merged with that for the Project Manager.

15 | Quality

Philosophy

Any thoughts or actions about quality in a project must start by finding out what the Customer's Quality Expectations are. It is dangerous to assume that the customer will always want a superb quality product that will last forever. Have a look at the products in your local cut-price store and you will see what I mean. Let me quote you two different examples of customer quality thinking from projects in my past.

A telecommunications company had bid for a packet switching system in Australia. They had been told they were the favoured supplier and their bid price looked good in relation to their competitors. Suddenly a bright young man employed by the Australian customer looked at the geography of the thing and said to his bosses, 'Most of this system is going to be across the deserted middle of the country. It's going to be very expensive to fix any faults out there. Have we specified a high enough quality?' So the tender was recalled and when it re-emerged it contained a quality requirement that said all components (hardware and software) supplied had to have a mean time between failure of three years. This was backed up by heavy penalty clauses in the event of failure. The bidding telecommunications company looked at its original bid, which had included testing work 'to a commercial level' and realised that this was not enough. So lots more testing, such as testing each hardware component to destruction, was added to the price, plus duplicate equipment to take over in case of failure, and so on. The price of their bid became so high that they lost the contract (but probably saved themselves money in the long run).

The exploration arm of an oil company came to their data processing section with the results of a seismic survey carried out in the mountains of a South American country. They had a very short time in which to analyse the results and decide if there were oil or gas reservoirs there. Their exploration contract had to be renewed or they would lose their favoured position. Their quality need was for accuracy of analysis. Beyond that they needed a fast turn-around. They weren't worried about the result layout being 'user-friendly'. The product was to be used once and then thrown away.

There is a big difference in the approach to quality needed by these two projects.

Overview

So project quality thinking starts with the Customer's Quality Expectations. After that it is likely that both the supplier and the customer will have quality standards already in place – a quality management system (QMS). Both may also have staff responsible for ensuring that these standards are used. Depending on the environment into which the final product will be delivered, there may be other standards to be reached. An example here would be a car's emission levels if we were building a new car. All of these need to be matched against the Customer's Quality Expectations, the anticipated project timeframe, the cost and the solution method. Out of this comparison we should get a list of the development standards, the testing methods and the tools to be used.

These quality requirements need to be related to the various products that the project will create or use. We then need to get down to putting into our detailed plans the work necessary to ensure that quality is built in, who will do this and when.

After this we need to consider an audit trail of our quality work. How do we prove to the customer that the necessary quality work has been done?

Detail

STEP	PRODUCT	PROCESS/ TECHNIQUE
Ascertain the Customer's Quality Expectations	Project Mandate or Project Brief	Starting Up a Project (SU)
Write a Project Quality Plan	Project Initiation Document	Initiating a Project
Write a Stage Quality Plan	Stage Plan	Managing Stage Boundaries
Define a product's quality criteria	Product Descriptions	Product-based Planning
Explain the quality requirements for each piece of work	Work Package	Controlling a Stage
Report back on the quality work performed	Quality Log	Managing Product Delivery
Check that quality work is being done correctly	Quality Review	Quality Review
Control changes	Project Issue	Change Control
Keep track of changes to products	Configuration records	Configuration management

CUSTOMER'S QUALITY EXPECTATIONS

The Customer's Quality Expectations should be made clear in the Project Mandate at the very outset of the project. If not sufficiently clear, the Project Manager should clarify the expectations when preparing the Project Brief (during 'Starting Up a Project' (SU)). The expectations should be measurable. 'Of good quality' may sound fine, but how can it be measured? Expectations of performance, reliability, flexibility, maintainability and capability can all be expressed in measurable terms.

Quality is one corner of a triangle as shown in Figure 15.1. The customer has to decide where, within the triangle, the project's main focus is to be. Does it incline more towards the cost, the time or the quality? This simple exercise shows that the three items are interlinked. If you want the product to be cheap, that may have an adverse effect on the quality, and so on.

Figure 15.1   The Quality, Cost and Time Triangle

THE PROJECT QUALITY PLAN

The next step is to decide how the project is going to meet the Customer's Quality Expectations for the product. Other inputs to this should be the standards to be used to guide the development of the product and test its ability to meet the quality expectations. The supplier should have standards, but the customer may also have standards that it insists on being used. Such standards have to be compared against the quality expectations to see which are to be used. There may be gaps where extra standards have to be obtained or created. The customer has the last say in what standards will be used to check the products. There may also be regulatory standards to be met.

The Project Quality Plan identifies the standards to be used and the main quality responsibilities. The latter may be a reference to a quality assurance function (belonging to either the customer, the supplier or both). There is a cross-reference here to the Project Board roles. These roles contain Project Assurance responsibility, many of them affecting quality. If these have been delegated, there must be a match with the responsibilities defined in the Project Quality Plan.

The Project Quality Plan refers to the establishment of the Quality Log, the quality file and their purposes.

The plan also identifies the procedures that will be used to control changes and the configuration management plan.

Product Descriptions are written for the key products shown in the Project Plan. These include specific quality criteria against which the products will be measured.

THE STAGE QUALITY PLAN

Each stage has its own quality plan containing lower level detail than the Project Quality Plan. This identifies the method of quality checking to be used for each product of the stage. The plan also identifies responsibility for each individual quality check. For example, for each Quality Review the chairman and reviewers are identified. This gives an opportunity for those with Project Assurance roles to see each draft Stage Plan and input its needs for checking and the staff who should represent it at each check.

Any major products developed in the stage have Product Descriptions written for them if they were not done as part of the Project Quality Plan.

Product Descriptions

A Product Description should be written for each major product to be produced by the project. The description should contain:

- Title

- Purpose

- Composition (what are the components of the product?)

- Derivation (what is the source of the components?)

- Format (what does the product have to look like?)

- Allocated to (what skills are needed for the product's creation?)

- Quality criteria (what quality does the product have to display?)

- Quality method (how will the product be tested so that it meets the quality criteria?)

- Quality checking skills required (what skills are needed to test the quality of the product?).

The Product Description should be written as soon as possible after the need for it is recognised. Writing the description helps the planner understand what the product is and how long it is likely to take to build it.

The Product Description is also the first place where we start thinking about the quality of the product, how we will test the presence of its quality and who we might need in order to test that quality.

It is very sensible to get the customer to write as much of the Product Description as possible, particularly its purpose and quality criteria. This helps the customer define what is needed and is useful when delivering a product to be able to confirm that a product meets its criteria.

The Product Description is an important part of the information handed to a Team Manager or individual as part of a Work Package.

Any time that a product that has been approved by the Project Board has to be changed, the Product Description should also be checked to see if it needs an update.

Quality File

The Project Manager should keep a file of all the quality checking information that is generated by the project. This forms an important audit trail for use by bodies such as customer or supplier quality assurance.

The quality file should contain the master copy of the Product Description, plus details of individual product test plans and a Quality Log. The Project Manager is responsible for setting up the quality file and Quality Log and checking that either Team Managers or individuals are feeding information into the log.

Quality Log

The Quality Log is a summary of tests planned and carried out, and test results. The initial entry is by the Project Manager when a Stage Plan is created. The Team Manager or individual adds the actual results as the quality checking is done.

Links

There is clearly a link to the project organisation. If the customer or supplier has an independent quality assurance function, how can they neatly fit into the project organisation? The answer is via the Project Assurance role. Both customer and supplier could appoint someone from their quality assurance function to carry out part of their Project Assurance role. This gives them access to the detailed planning, when they can ensure that satisfactory testing with the correct participants has been planned. They can get feedback from these participants either directly or through the Quality Log about the results of quality work.

The Project Assurance function can do a valuable job by checking that the Product Descriptions are correct.

Clearly change control has an impact on quality. If uncontrolled changes are made this is likely to destroy the quality of the project in terms of schedule and costs, as well as making it unclear what is being delivered. This means that there would be no connection between what was originally requested and what is finally delivered.

In the same way configuration management has links to quality. If you do not keep control over what version of a product you are using, the quality is likely to suffer.

Do's and Don'ts

Do treat the need for quality very seriously. The customer may, over time, forgive you for delivering late and may forgive you for coming in over budget. But the customer will never forgive you for delivering a poor quality product.

Don't miss out on any of the quality steps.

If it's a Large Project

Quality is like carpet underlay. It enhances the feel and life of the product, but it is very difficult to put it in afterwards. In a large project, you can't check everyone's work. Make full use of the Project Assurance role to check for you. Your job is to define the quality required, plan for it, monitor people who are checking for it and react quickly if there is a quality problem.

Where you have several teams working for you, ensure that the Project Assurance roles check the quality work intentions in the Team Plans and get customer people in there, checking that the supplier is delivering good quality. Finding out during acceptance testing that a poor quality solution has been delivered is far too late. All too often this leads to litigation and only the lawyers win there. Remember, the customer doesn't want large penalty payments. The customer wants a product that will meet the requirements.

If it's a Small Project

It is very easy to think that quality in a small project will look after itself. 'It's such a small project, we can check the quality when we've finished. Delivering a quality product from a small project is easy', they will say. 'Only an idiot could get it wrong.' Well, if you don't go through the quality steps mentioned above, it could be 'welcome to the idiot's club'.

16 | Risk

Philosophy

Risk can be defined as uncertainty of outcome (whether positive opportunity or negative threat). Some amount of risk taking is inevitable if the project is to achieve its objectives. Projects bring about change, and change incurs risk. Change is usually about moving forward, and this often means the use of new methods, new technology. These can increase the risks.

Risk can also be formally defined as:

> *the chance of exposure to the adverse consequences of future events.*

It is not uncommon to hear people say 'This is a high risk project.' This statement by itself is of limited interest or value. We need far more detail. What are the actual risks? What are their causes? What is the probability of the risk occurring? How serious would the impact of that occurrence be? What can be done about it?

There are many methods of risk management on the market and quite a few software packages that will help you with a standard set of questions and 'forms' to come to a view of the risk situation of your project. To my mind, far more important than which method you choose is **when** should you carry out assessment of risk. Too many projects look at the risk situation at the beginning of a project, then forget about it for the rest of the project (or until a risk comes up and smacks them on the jaw!).

In summary I suggest that you:

- Carry out risk assessment at the start of a project. Make proposals on what should be done about the risks. Get agreement on whether to start the project or not.

- Review the risks at the end of every stage. This includes existing risks that might have changed and new risks caused by the next Stage Plan. Get agreement on whether to continue into the next stage.

- Appoint an owner for every risk. Build into the Stage Plan the moments when the owners should be monitoring the risks. Check on the owners to see that they are doing the job and keeping the risk status up to date.

- Review every request for change for its impact on existing risks or the creation of a new risk. Build the time and cost of any risk avoidance or reduction, for example, into your recommendation on the action to be taken.

- Inspect the risks at the end of the project for any that might affect the product in its operational life. If there are any, make sure that you notify those charged with looking after the product. (Use the Follow-on Action Recommendations for this.)

These points should be enough for you to keep control of the risk situation. If you have very long stages (which I do not recommend) and very few requests for change, you may decide to review risks on a monthly basis.

There is one other point of philosophy about risk. When considering actions, you have to consider the cost of taking action against the cost of not taking action.

Overview

The aim of management of risk is to assess a project's exposure to risk (that is, the probability of specific risks occurring and the potential impact if they did occur), and manage that exposure by taking action to keep exposure to an acceptable level in a cost-effective way.

Identification and decisions about risks at project level form an important part of the Business Case. Where suppliers and/or partners are involved, for example, it is important to gain a shared view of the risks and how they will be managed.

Where the project is part of a programme, there must be a common view of all risks at programme level. A risk or an action to counter a project risk might have an undesired effect on the programme or another project in the programme.

Risk Tolerance

Before deciding what to do about risks, a project must consider the amount of risk it can tolerate. The view of how much the project is prepared to put at risk will depend on a number of variables. A project may be prepared to take comparatively large risks in some areas and none at all in others, such as risks to company survival, exceeding budgets or target date, fulfilling health and safety regulations. Another name for risk tolerance is 'risk appetite'.

Risk tolerance can be related to the four tolerance parameters; risk to completion within timescale and/or cost, and to achieving product quality and project scope within the boundaries of the Business Case.

Risk tolerances have to be considered carefully to obtain the optimum balance of the cost of a risk occurring against the cost of limiting or preventing that risk. The organisation's overall risk tolerance must also be considered as well as that of the project.

Risk Responsibilities

The management of risk is one of the most important tasks of the Project Board and the Project Manager. The Project Manager is responsible for ensuring that risks are identified, recorded and regularly reviewed. The Project Board has four responsibilities:

1. Notifying the Project Manager of any external risk exposure to the project

2. Making decisions on the Project Manager's recommended reactions to risk

3. Striking a balance between level of risk and the potential benefits that the project may achieve

4. Notifying corporate or programme management of any risks that affect the project's ability to meet corporate or programme constraints.

The Project Manager modifies plans to include agreed actions to avoid or reduce the impact of risks.

Risk analysis requires input from the management of the organisation. The organisation's management, in turn, is kept informed by the Project Board of the risk status.

Risk Ownership

The person best situated to keep an eye on a risk should be identified as its 'owner'. The Project Manager will normally suggest the 'owner' and the Project Board should confirm the decision. Project Board members may be appointed 'owners' of risks, particularly risks from sources external to the project.

The Risk Management Process

See Figure 16.1.

RISK ANALYSIS

Risk Identification

This step identifies the potential risks (or opportunities) facing the project. It is important not to judge the likelihood of a risk at this early time. This is done in a controlled manner in a later step. Attempting to form judgements whilst 'brainstorming' a list of potential risks may lead to hurried and incorrect decisions to exclude some risks.

Once identified, risks are all entered in the Risk Log. This is a summary document of all risks, their assessment, owners and status.

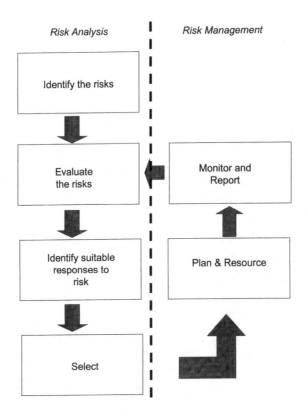

Figure 16.1   The Management of Risk Cycle

The Risk Log is a control tool for the Project Manager, providing a quick reference to the key risks facing the project, what monitoring activities should be taking place and by whom. Reference to it can lead to entries in the Project Manager's Daily Log to check on a risk.

Evaluation

Risk evaluation is concerned with assessing probability of a risk occurring and the impact if it does occur.

Impact should ideally be considered under the elements of:

- Time

- Quality

- Benefit

- People.

For example, a major fire in a building is relatively unlikely to happen, but would have enormous impact on business continuity. Conversely, occasional car breakdowns are fairly likely to happen, but would not usually have a major impact on the business.

Some risks, such as financial risk, can be evaluated in numerical terms. Others, such as adverse publicity, can only be evaluated in subjective ways. There is a need for some measurement of risks. This manual uses **high**, **medium** and **low**.

When considering a risk's probability, another aspect is when the risk might occur or when risk actions need to be considered. Some risks will be predicted to be further away in time than others, and so attention can be focused on the more immediate ones. This prediction is called the risk's proximity. The proximity of each risk should be included in the Risk Log.

Identify Suitable Responses to Risk

There are five types of action:

Prevention	Terminate the risk – by doing things differently and thus removing the risk. Countermeasures are put in place that either stop the threat or problem from occurring, or prevent it having any impact on the project or business

Reduction	Treat the risk – take action to control it in some way where the actions either reduce the likelihood of the risk developing or limit the impact on the project to acceptable levels
Transference	This is a specialist form of risk reduction where the impact of the risk is passed to a third party via, for instance, an insurance policy or penalty clause
Acceptance	Tolerate the risk – perhaps because nothing can be done at a reasonable cost to mitigate it, or the likelihood and impact of the risk occurring are at an acceptable level
Contingency	These are actions planned and organised to come into force as and when the risk occurs

A risk may have appropriate actions in more than one of the above categories.

The results of the risk evaluation activities are documented in the Risk Log. If the project is part of a programme, project risks should be examined for any impact on the programme (and vice versa). Where any cross-impact is found, the risk should be added to the other Risk Log.

Selection

The selection step involves identifying and evaluating a range of options for treating risks and preparing and implementing risk management plans. It is important that the control action put in place is proportional to the risk. Every control has an associated cost. The control action must offer better value for money than the risk that it is controlling. See Figure 16.20.

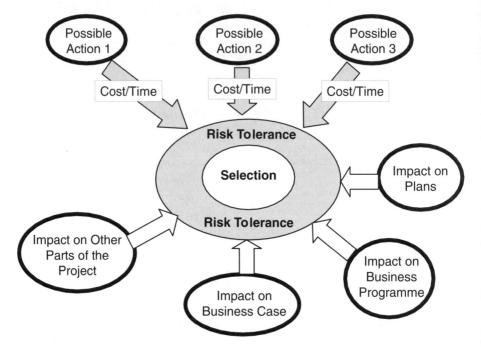

Figure 16.2   Risk Action Selection

There may be several possible risk actions, each with different effects. The choice may be one of these options or a combination of two or more. We then have to consider the impact of (a) the risk occurring and (b) the risk action on:

- The Team, Stage and/or Project Plans
- The business or programme
- The Business Case
- Other parts of the project.

The consideration has to be done in the light of the risk tolerances.

RISK MANAGEMENT

Planning and Resourcing

Having made the selection, the implementation will need planning and resourcing, and is likely to include plan changes and new or modified Work Packages:

1. Planning, which consists of:

    *   Identifying the quantity and type of resources required to carry out the actions

    *   Developing a detailed plan of action

    *   Confirming the desirability of carrying out the actions in light of any additional information gained

    *   Obtaining management approval.

2. Resourcing, which will identify and assign the actual resources to be used to do the work to carry out the risk counteractions. These assignments will be shown in Stage and Team Plans. Note that resources required for the prevention, reduction and transference actions will have to be funded from the project budget, since they are actions the project is committed to carry out. Contingent actions will normally be funded from a contingency budget.

Monitoring and Reporting

There must be mechanisms in place for monitoring and reporting on the actions selected to address risks.

Some of the actions may have only been to monitor the identified risk for signs of a change in its status. Monitoring, however, may consist of:

1. Checking that execution of the planned actions is having the desired effect

2. Watching for the early warning signs that a risk is developing

3. Modelling trends, predicting potential risks or opportunities

4. Checking that the overall management of risk is being applied effectively.

Normally the risk 'owner' will have the responsibility of monitoring. If the owner is a Project Board member, the actual task of monitoring may be delegated, but the responsibility stays with the owner. The Executive, for example, has ultimate responsibility for monitoring any risks or opportunities facing the Business Case, particularly any external ones, such as changes in company policy. The Project Manager has the job of keeping a watching brief over all risks and checking that the defined actions, including monitoring, are taking place and are having the desired effect.

Risks owned at team level should be reported in the Checkpoint Reports. The Project Manager includes some form of report on any significant risks in the Highlight Report. The End Stage Report also summarises the risk status. Where a risk or opportunity actually occurs, a Project Issue should be used to trigger the necessary actions.

Budgeting for the Management of Risk

A project needs to allocate the appropriate budget, time and resources to the management of risk. The cost of carrying out the risk process and the level of commitment and time, such as contingency plans, risk avoidance or reduction, need to be recognised and agreed. Whilst budget may be allocated to actions relating to risk treatment, there is often a failure to provide sufficient budget to the earlier parts of the process, such as risk assessment that can require a diverse range of skills, tools and techniques. Experience has shown that allocating enough budget to the risk process early on will pay dividends later.

Mapping the Risk Management Process to the PRINCE2 Processes

At key points in a project, management of risk should be carried out (Figure 16.3).

PREPARING A PROJECT BRIEF (FOCUSING ON BUSINESS RISKS) (SU4)

The Risk Log needs to be created by this time. The Project Mandate may have referred to a number of risks facing the potential project. These may be such risks as competitor action, impending or mooted legislation, company policy changes, staff reorganisation or cash flow problems. Certainly, the preparation of the Project Brief should give rise to an early study of such risks. Creation of the Project Approach may also have introduced some extra risks.

AUTHORISING INITIATION (DP1)

This is the first formal moment when the Project Board can examine the Risk Log as part of deciding whether project initiation can be justified. Pragmatically, the Project Manager should have discussed informally with board members any known risks that seem to threaten the project viability.

REFINING THE BUSINESS CASE AND RISKS (FOCUSING ON BOTH BUSINESS AND PROJECT RISKS) (IP3)

The Project Manager examines risks again as part of preparing the Project Initiation Document. At this time the Project Plan will have been created, and this may identify a number of project risks, such as lack of resources, contractor ability and any assumptions being made in the plan. New risks may also come to light as a result of adding detail to the Project Brief. At the same time all existing risks are reviewed for any new information or change in their circumstances.

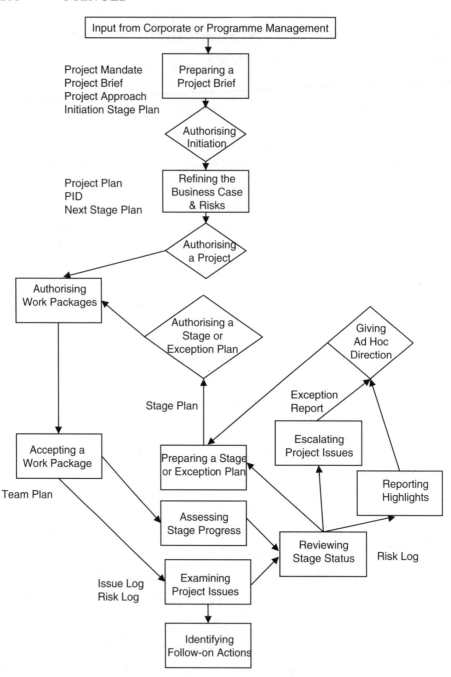

Figure 16.3   Risk Flow, Showing Key Points in a Project When Management is Necessary

AUTHORISING A PROJECT (DP2)

The Project Board now has an updated Risk Log to examine as part of its decision on whether to go ahead with the project. As a result of refining the Business Case, a number of extra risks may have been identified. Very often the 'owners' of these risks will be members of the Project Board, and they should confirm their ownership and the actions required of them.

PLANNING (PL)

Each time a plan is produced, elements of the plan may identify new risks, modify existing ones or eliminate others. No plan should be put forward for approval before its risk content has been analysed. This analysis may lead to the plan being modified in order to take the appropriate risk action(s). The Risk Log should be updated with all such details.

UPDATING THE RISK LOG (SB4)

As part of the preparation for a new stage, the Project Manager updates the Risk Log with any changes to existing risks.

AUTHORISING A STAGE OR EXCEPTION PLAN (DP3)

Before authorising a plan, the Project Board has the opportunity to study the risk situation as part of its judgement of the continuing viability of the project.

AUTHORISING WORK PACKAGE (CS1)

Negotiation with the Team Manager or team member may identify new risks or change old ones. It may require the Project Manager to go back and amend some part of the original Work Package or change the Stage Plan. Examples here are the assignee seeking more time or needing to change resources.

ACCEPTING A WORK PACKAGE (MP1)

This is the point when the Team Manager makes out a Team Plan to ensure that the products of the Work Package can be delivered within the constraints of the agreed Work Package. Like any other plan, it may contain new risks or modify existing ones.

EXAMINING PROJECT ISSUES (CS4)

Assessment of a new Project Issue may throw up a risk situation. This may stem from either the technical impact analysis or the business impact analysis. For example, the proposed change may produce a risk of pushing the stage or project beyond its tolerance margins.

REVIEWING STAGE STATUS (CS5)

This brings together the Stage Plan with its latest actual figures, the Project Plan, the Business Case, open Project Issues, the tolerance status and the Risk Log. The Project Manager in conjunction with the Project Assurance roles looks for risk situation changes as well as any other warning signs.

The Project Manager's Daily Log can be very useful in monitoring risks. Entries can be made in it for the Project Manager to check on the status of any risks where he/she is the owner. Other entries can be made to remind the Project Manager to check that other owners are monitoring their risks and feeding the information back.

ESCALATING PROJECT ISSUES (CS8)

As well as Project Issues, a risk change may cause the Project Manager to raise an Exception Report to the Project Board.

REPORTING HIGHLIGHTS (CS6)

As part of this task, the Project Manager may take the opportunity to raise any risk matters with the Project Board. Examples here would be notifying the board of any risks that are no longer relevant, warning about new risks, and reminders about business risks that board members should be keeping an eye on. The suggested format of a Highlight Report is included in Appendix 1.

GIVING AD HOC DIRECTION (DP4)

The Project Manager advises the Project Board of exception situations via the Exception Report. The board has the opportunity to react with advice or a decision – for example, bringing the project to a premature close, requesting an Exception Plan, or removing the problem. The Project Board may instigate ad hoc advice on the basis of information given to it from corporate or programme management or another external source.

IDENTIFYING FOLLOW-ON ACTIONS (CP2)

At the end of the project a number of risks may have been identified that will affect the product in its operational life. These should be transferred to the Follow-on Action Recommendations for the information of those who will support the product after the project.

It should be recognised that it may be desirable to accept some risks in order to obtain additional benefits to the project. **Note**: the option to take no action may sometimes be appropriate. This means that a decision is made that the perceived level of risk is acceptable.

How effectively a risk can be managed depends on the identification of its underlying causes and the amount of control that the project management team can exert over those causes. It is more effective to reduce the potential cause of a risk than to wait for that risk to materialise and then address its impact.

The impact of a risk that materialises should not be mistaken for the underlying cause of the risk. For example, **cost escalation** on a project is an ever-present risk impact. Expenditure should be monitored to determine the underlying causes of **why** costs are escalating.

It is important that the management of risk is considered as a continuous process throughout the life of a project. Once potential risks have been identified they need to be monitored until such time as either they cease to be material, or their effect has been reduced or mitigated as a result of management intervention. The potential for new risks being introduced with time, or in consequence of actions taken, also needs to be considered throughout the project life cycle.

Illustrative List of Risk Analysis Questions

This section contains an illustrative list of questions that a Project Manager may require to have answered for a particular project. It is based on the OGC publication, 'Management of Project Risk'.

BUSINESS/STRATEGIC

1. Do the project objectives fit into the organisation's overall business strategy?

2. When is the project due to deliver; how was the date determined?

3. What would be the result of late delivery?

4. What would be the result of limited success (functionality)?

5. What is the stability of the business area?

EXTERNAL FACTORS

1. Is this project exposed to requirements due to international interests (i.e. are there legal implications from overseas, or are foreign companies involved)?

2. Could there be 'political' implications of the project failing?

3. Is this project part of a programme? If so, what constraints are set for the project by that programme?

PROCUREMENT

1. Has the supplier a reputation for delivery of high quality goods?

2. Is the contract sufficiently detailed to show what the supplier is going to provide?

3. Are the acceptance criteria clear to both parties?

4. Is the contract legally binding/enforceable? (Consideration should be given to topics including ownership rights and liability.)

ORGANISATIONAL FACTORS

1. What consideration needs to be given to security for this project?

2. Does the project have wholehearted support from senior management?

3. What is the commitment of the user management?

4. Have training requirements been identified? Can these requirements be met?

MANAGEMENT

1. How clearly are the project objectives defined?

2. Will the project be run using a well-documented approach to project management?

3. Does this approach cover aspects of quality management, risk and development activities in sufficient depth?

4. How well do the project team understand the chosen methodology?

5. What is the current state of Project Plans?

6. Is completion of this project dependent on the completion of other projects?

7. Are the tasks in the Project Plan interdependent (and can the critical path through tasks be identified)?

8. What is the availability of appropriate resources? (What are the skills and experience of the project team? What is the make-up of the project team?)

9. Will people be available for training? (For IS projects this includes the project team, users and operations staff.)

10. How many separate user functions are involved?

11. How much change will there be to the users' operation or organisation?

TECHNICAL

1. Is the specification clear, concise, accurate and feasible?

2. How have the technical options been evaluated?

3. What is the knowledge of the equipment (for IT, for example, this is the hardware/software environment)?

4. Does the experience of the Project Manager cover a similar application?

5. Is this a new application?

6. What is the complexity of the system?

7. How many sites will the system be implemented in?

8. Is the proposed equipment new/leading edge? Is the proposed hardware/software environment in use already?

9. Who is responsible for defining system testing?

10. Who is responsible for defining acceptance testing?

11. On what basis is the implementation planned?

12. What access will the project team have to the development facilities?

13. Will the user or specialist staff operate the system?

14. Have requirements for long-term operations, maintenance and support been identified?

Links

There are many links to the PRINCE2 processes, as described under the heading 'Mapping the risk management process to the PRINCE2 processes'. In addition we can consider the following links.

THE PLANNING PROCESS

When a draft plan has been produced, it should be examined for risks before being published.

CAPTURING PROJECT ISSUES (CS3)

When a risk actually happens, transferring the risk to a Project Issue triggers the necessary action. The reason is simple. There is already a well-defined action process to handle problems in the change control procedure. Why create another one just for risks? The Risk Log is marked with a cross-reference to the Project Issue. The Project Issue is cross-referenced to the risk in the Risk Log. Then we continue with impact analysis and the various options in change control.

TAKING CORRECTIVE ACTION (CS7)

If a risk status becomes worse, the Project Manager may be able to take corrective action within the tolerance limits.

Do's and Don'ts

Do examine every plan for risks before publishing it.

Do appoint an owner for every risk.

Do try to delegate as many of these as possible. When writing up your Daily Log for actions to take next week, do look at the Risk Log to find owners who should be reporting on the status of risks.

Don't forget to warn the Project Board of any risk deterioration that might go beyond the tolerance margins.

Don't be shy about appointing a member of the Project Board as owner of a risk.

If it's a Large Project

Some large organisations now employ a Risk Manager, an expert/consultant who advises all Project Managers on identifying and controlling risks.

It is sensible to set aside some time specifically to consider the risk situation. This will be a natural part of each stage boundary, but in a long project it is also worth setting this time aside, say, every two weeks.

If it's a Small Project

Risks are still an important factor.

17 | Change Control

Philosophy

No matter how well planned a project has been, if there is no control over changes, this will destroy any chance of bringing the project in on schedule and to budget. In any project there will be changes for many reasons:

- Government legislation has changed and this must be reflected in the product specification

- The users change their mind on what is wanted

- Because the development cycle is making the user think more and more about the product, extra features suggest themselves for inclusion

- There is a merge of departments, change of responsibility, company merger or takeover, which radically alters the project definition

- The supplier finds that it will be impossible to deliver everything within the agreed schedule or cost

- The supplier cannot meet an acceptance criterion, such as performance

- A product delivered by an outside contractor or another project fails to meet its specification.

All of these need a procedure to control them and their effect on the project. This procedure must make sure they are not ignored, but that nothing is implemented of which the appropriate level of management is unaware. This includes the Project Board.

Overview

A Project Issue is the formal way into a project of any inquiry, complaint or request (outside the scope of a Quality Review Question List). It can be raised by anyone associated with the project about anything, for example:

- A desired new or changed function

- A failure of a product in meeting some aspect of the user requirements. In such cases the report should be accompanied by evidence of the failure and, where appropriate, sufficient material to allow someone to recreate the failure for assessment purposes

- A question about a possible misunderstanding

- A problem with a plan

- A failure of communication.

In other words, there is no limit to the content of a Project Issue beyond the fact that it should be about the project.

Any error found during a Quality Review normally goes on a QR Action List. There are two exceptions to this:

- Where an error is found during Quality Review which belongs to a different product than the one under review

- Where work to correct an error found during Quality Review cannot be done during the agreed follow-up period.

Such errors are put onto a Project Issue as a way of getting them into the change control system.

When considering the procedures for handling Project Issues, there is the possibility that the subject will be outside the scope of the project. An example might be a fault in a component that is used in many products across the department. Although it is being used in the project it clearly has a wider implication. There should be a procedure to close the issue off as far as the project is concerned and transfer it to a departmental level. The same approach applies if the project is part of a programme and an error is found in a Quality Review that affects other projects in the programme.

All possible changes should be handled by the same change control procedure. Apart from controlling possible changes, this procedure should provide a formal entry point through which questions or suggestions also can be raised and answered.

Detail

We shall consider three types of Project Issue:

- Requests for Change
- Off-Specifications
- Questions or suggestions.

CHANGE CONTROL PROCEDURE

The Configuration Librarian will log receipt of the Project Issue, allocate the unique identifier, and pass a copy back to the originator and to the Project Manager. The Project Issue is now classed as 'Open'.

The Project Manager allocates the issue to the person or team best suited to examine it. The issues are evaluated with the aim of making recommendations to the Project Manager on their resolution. The outcome is normally one of the following (see Figure 17.1):

- The issue has been raised because of a misunderstanding by the originator. The misunderstanding should be explained to the originator and the issue closed.

- The issue is proposing a change to a baselined configuration item. The Project Issue is a Request for Change and the decision can only be made by the Project Board (or Change Authority if one has been appointed – see SU2).

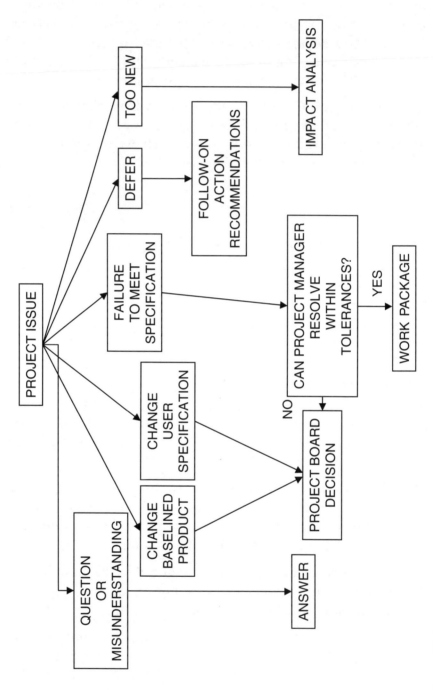

Figure 17.1

- The issue requests a change to the agreed user specification, acceptance criteria or a Product Description. The Project Issue is a Request for Change and the decision can only be made by the Project Board (or Change Authority if one has been appointed – see SU2).

- A product does not meet its specification. The Project Issue is an Off-Specification.

- The issue should be deferred to a later enhancement project.

- The issue was received too recently for any evaluation.

The Project Manager should review all open issues. He or she may do this alone, with a senior technical member of the team and/or with those carrying Project Assurance responsibility. The frequency of such meetings will depend on the volume of issues being received, but they should be held regularly and with sufficient frequency to ensure that no inordinate delay occurs in taking action.

All Project Issues have to be closed by the end of the project or transferred to the Follow-on Action Recommendations. The transfer of a Project Issue to these recommendations can only be done with the approval of the Project Board.

REQUEST FOR CHANGE

A request for change records a proposed modification to the user requirements.

The request for change requires analysis to see how much work is involved. Senior team members with the appropriate skills and experience normally do this. Part of this work is called impact analysis, where the configuration library holds information that will help to identify what other products or configuration items will be affected. It is particularly important that the librarian identifies any baselined configuration items that will need to change. This is because the Project Board has already been told of the completion of those items. The Project Board must approve any change to such items.

The identified work is costed and the impact on the Stage Plan's budget and schedule assessed. For the next decision the Project Manager will want to know if any of the work could be done within the tolerance levels of the current plan. For this reason it is best that a batch of requests is studied, to give a wider view of the effect on the plans.

In preparation for the next decision, the Requests for Change have to be awarded a priority rating. This can be one of four:

- High
- Medium
- Low
- Cosmetic.

It should be the job of the users to provide the priority rating.

In order for the Request for Change to be implemented, it must be approved by either the Project Manager or the Project Board. Whose decision it is depends on the following:

- If it is not a change to a configuration item that has already been **baselined** and the work can be done within the current plan's **tolerances**, the Project Manager **can** make the decision to implement it. Alternatively it can be passed to the Project Board (or Change Authority if one has been appointed – see SU2) for its decision. Since experience shows that there will be a lot of changes during the project, it is a good idea to make the Project Board decide on any changes other than trivialities. This keeps the Board aware of how many changes are being requested and their cumulative impact on the schedule and cost. If the Stage Plan runs into trouble later, it is usually too late for the Project Manager to get any sympathy about a claim that lots of requests have been actioned without asking for more time or money. The answer will usually be 'Why didn't you ask us? We could have cancelled or delayed some of them.'

- The decision must be made by the Project Board (or Change Authority if one has been appointed – see SU2) if the change is to one or more configuration items that the Project Board has already been told are complete (to any baseline, not necessarily the final one). More than anything, this is to retain the confidence level of the Board. If it has been told that something is finished and later finds out that it has been changed without consultation, its sense of being in control evaporates.

- If the work to do the Request for Change cannot be done within the tolerance levels of the current Stage Plan, the decision on action **must** come from the Project Board. The Project Manager must submit an Exception Plan with the Request for Change, showing the new schedule and cost for the rest of the stage.

If the Project Board retains the authority, then all those requests for change that have not been decided by the Project Manager are passed to the Project Board.

The Project Board's decision may be to:

- Implement the change. If the change requires an Exception Plan, then this means approving the Exception Plan

- Delay the change to an enhancement project after the current one is finished

- Defer a decision until a later meeting

- Ask for more information

- Cancel the request.

If the Project Board has delegated the responsibility for decision on Project Issues to a Change Authority, then the Change Authority will play the role described above. The decision should be documented on the Project Issue and in the Issue Log.

Whenever its status changes, a copy of the updated Project Issue should be sent to the originator.

The Project Manager is responsible for scheduling any approved changes. This work will possibly involve the issue of a new version of one or more products by the Configuration Librarian.

On receipt of a completed Request for Change the Configuration Librarian should ensure that any amended products have been resubmitted to the configuration library. The finalised request should be stored in the quality file, and the originator advised.

OFF-SPECIFICATION

An Off-Specification is used to document any situation where the product is failing to meet its specification in some respect.

The Configuration Librarian allocates the next unique Project Issue identifier from the Issue Log and sends a copy of the issue to its author. Senior team members carry out an impact analysis with the help of the Configuration Librarian to discover which products are affected by the Off-Specification, and then assess the effort needed.

As with Requests for Change, the decision on action is taken by either the Project Manager or Project Board (or a Change Authority appointed by the Project Board). If the error is because of a failure within the Project Manager's responsibility, the onus is on the Project Manager to correct the problem within tolerances. Similarly, if the error is from a Team Manager's failure to fulfil an agreed Work Package, the onus is on the Team Manager (or the supplier if the team is from an external company) to correct the error without asking the Project Manager for more time or money.

- If the Off-Specification does not involve a change to a configuration item that has already been baselined and the work can be done within the current plan's tolerances, the Project Manager should make the decision to implement it.

- If the Off-Specification requires changes to one or more configuration items which the Project Board has already been told are complete (to any baseline, not necessarily the final one), the Project Board must make the decision.

- If the work to do the Off-Specification cannot be done within the tolerance levels of the current Stage Plan, the decision on action must come from the Project Board. The Project Manager will write an Exception Report and send it to the Project Board with the Off-Specification, showing the new schedule and cost for the rest of the stage.

The Project Board's decision may be to:

- Correct the fault. If the work required an Exception Plan, then this means approving the Exception Plan

- Delay correction of the fault to an enhancement project after the current one is finished

- Defer a decision until a later meeting

- Ask for more information.

The decision should be documented on the Off-Specification and the Issue Log, and an updated copy filed. Again, whenever it is updated, a copy of the Project Issue should be sent to the originator.

The Project Manager is responsible for scheduling any approved work to correct Off-Specifications. This work will possibly involve the issue of a new version of one or more products by the Configuration Librarian.

On receipt of a corrected Off-Specification the Configuration Librarian should ensure that any amended products have been resubmitted to the configuration library. The Issue Log should be updated with the final details and the originator advised.

THE QUALITY FILE

There is one quality file for each project. It is the responsibility of the Project Manager. If a Configuration Librarian has been appointed to the project it is important that the duties with regard to the quality file are clearly defined between this role and the Project Manager. Normally the Configuration Librarian will be allocated the duties of logging and filing all the documents.

The quality file contains the Quality Log and the forms that are produced as part of the quality controls applied during the life of the project. It is an important part of the audit trail that can be followed by the user or an independent quality assurance body to assess what quality checking has been carried out and how effective it has been. As such, it is a deliverable product.

Wherever possible, the originals of documents should be filed in the quality file. A copy can be filed if the original has to be circulated for signature or comments, but on its return the original should be replaced in the quality file.

The quality file should have sections for:

- Quality Log
  Each quality check should have a unique number to provide the basis for statistics on how many quality checks have been carried out.

- Quality Review Invitations
  On filing this document there should be a check that there is no unreported date slippage compared to the planned review date. If there is, the Project Manager should be notified.

- Quality Review Results
  When all corrective actions on the Action List have been taken and the list signed off by the chairman of the review, it is filed in the quality file. If the review was terminated prematurely, the review documents such as follow-up Action List, annotated product copies, Question Lists should all be filed here in the quality file.

- Issue Log.

Links

There is a very strong link between change control and configuration management. Any new version of a product should have a link to the Project Issue that caused the creation of the new version. It is sensible to give the same person or group responsibility for change control and configuration management.

There is another link with organisation and the 'Initiating a Project' process. Before the project begins there should be a decision on how big the change control need is likely to be and what part of the project management team will administer change control. Will it be a member of the team, part time? Will an administrative clerk come in for half a day a week? Does it need a small group of specialist Configuration Librarians?

Another link is between 'Starting Up a Project', the organisation, plans and change control. At the outset of a project a decision is needed on whether a change authority is needed and how changes will be funded.

Do's and Don'ts

Do think about the stability of the customer's specification before you dive into a project. The less stable it is, the more change control will be required and the higher the cost of authorised changes is likely to be.

Don't underestimate the importance of change control. There is no project control without it.

If it's a Large Project

There may be many changes, so many that the Project Board cannot find the time to consider them all. They can choose to appoint a change authority, a group of people representing the Project Board, particularly the user side. The change authority will meet at a frequency based on the volume of changes coming through. In order for the change authority to operate, the Project Board will allocate it a change budget and provide certain restrictions. These may be the maximum amount of the budget to be spent in one stage and the maximum amount of the budget that can be spent on one change.

If it's a Small Project

Change control will still be important.

18	# Configuration Management

Philosophy

No organisation can be fully efficient or effective unless it manages its assets, particularly if the assets are vital to the running of the organisation's business. A project's assets likewise have to be managed. The assets of the project are the products that it develops. The name for the combined set of these assets is a configuration. The configuration of the final deliverable of a project is the sum total of its products.

In the foreword to its Product Configuration Management System (PCMS), SQL Software wrote 'If the product you develop has more than one version, more than a few components or more than one person working on it, you are doing Configuration Management. The only question is how well you are doing it.'

Overview

Within the context of project management the purpose of configuration management is to identify, track and protect the project's products as they are developed.

The objective of configuration management is to achieve a controlled and traceable product evolution through properly authorised specifications, design, development and testing.

This objective is met by defining and ensuring:

- The issue and control of properly authorised specifications

- The issue and control of properly authorised design documents

- The issue and control of properly authorised changes to the specification or design documents

- The control of the various versions of a product and their relationship with its current state.

Configuration management is also the process of managing change to the components that comprise a product. It implies that any version of the product and any revision of the components that make up the product can be retrieved at any time, and that the resulting product will always be built in an identical manner. Product enhancements and special variants create the need to control multiple versions and releases of the product. All these have to be handled by configuration management.

Configuration management is a discipline which:

- Records what components or products are required in order to build a product

- Provides identifiers and version numbers to all products

- Controls access and change to components of a product once they have been declared complete by the developer

- Provides information on the impact of possible changes

- Keeps information on the links between the various parts of a product, e.g. what components comprise a product, where is component X used, of what does the 'full product' consist

- Provides information on the status of products (Configuration Items) being developed, including who is responsible for the development

- Is the sensible storage place for Product Descriptions

- Gives project management the assurance that products are being developed in the correct sequence.

Configuration management holds a central position in project management. Product Breakdown Structures used in planning provide the information for the identified configuration items and their life cycles. The links allow the construction of the Product Flow Diagrams. They offer input and verification of the products required for a plan. You cannot adequately do change control without configuration management. It provides product copies and Product Descriptions for quality checks and keeps track of the status of the product. It provides the information to construct a release package, either a complete one or a partial one, and then records the issue of a release.

Configuration items are valuable assets in themselves. Configuration management helps management know what its assets are supposed to be, who is responsible for their safekeeping and whether the actual inventory matches the official one.

Configuration management gives control over the versions of products in use, identifies products affected by any problems, and makes it easier to assess the impact of changes.

Configuration management supports the production of information on problem trends, such as which products are being changed regularly or frequently, thereby assisting in the proactive prevention of problems.

Where the end product is to be used in more than one place, configuration management helps organisations to control the distribution of changes to these operational sites. Where there is any volume of changes, there will be the need to decide between putting together a 'release package' of several changes or issuing a complete new product. The latter may be a more controlled and cost-effective means of updating an operational product than sending out one changed product at a time. The decision and control mechanisms for this are part of configuration management.

Configuration management supports the maintenance of information on proven reliable releases to which products can revert in case of problems.

Because all products are under the control of configuration management once they have been developed, it makes it more difficult for them to be changed maliciously, thus improving security.

The data held in the configuration library help to recreate a release after any disaster by identifying the products required and their storage place.

Detail

Configuration management covers all the technical products of a project. It can also be used to record and store management and quality products, such as plans, quality check details and approvals to proceed. Whether management products are included or not depends on a number of factors such as:

- Effort involved

- Resource availability

- Capability of any other current method for handling management and quality products

- Project Manager's preference

- Availability of configuration management software.

COSTS

There are the expected costs of staffing and training Configuration Librarians. If a central office (say part of a project support office) has been set up to provide configuration management functions to a number of projects, there may be a need for a configuration manager.

If software is to be used to record and track the data, there will be the cost of its purchase or rental, any hardware bought to run it, plus the staff training. Having said that, it is very difficult to keep the comprehensive records required to do a complete job without a computer database and software. The costs here are far outweighed by the increase in speed, capacity and detail of information. The increase in speed of reaction by the Configuration Librarian probably reduces the number of librarians needed to cover all the site's products.

The need to go through the configuration management tasks may slow down slightly the handover of a finished item or the implementation of a change. But this penalty is very small when weighed against the risk and impact of operationally using a product that is from an incorrect release, or has not been checked out. Without it there is also the risk of more than one person changing a product simultaneously, resulting in all but the final change being lost.

POSSIBLE PROBLEMS

If products are defined at too low a level, the Configuration Librarian may be overwhelmed by the amount of data to be fed into the library. This is particularly a problem where no configuration management software is being used.

If products are defined at too high a level, the information for impact analysis may be too vague and result in a larger than necessary product change being indicated, e.g. altering a whole set of products when only one product is affected.

Procedures must cater for emergency changes, where an emergency change is required in order to let the operational product continue.

Where configuration management is new, development staff may be tempted to view its controls as bottlenecks and bureaucracy. But it has been used in engineering for many years and is regarded in those circles as essential. It is also regarded as an essential part of any quality product, should you be looking for accreditation under such standards as ISO 9000. It is regarded as essential because of the control it gives and experience over many years, which has shown its value and the cost of problems arising when it is not used.

WHEN IS IT DONE?

A Configuration Management Plan is required as part of the Project Quality Plan in the PID. This should state:

- What method is to be used

- Who has the responsibility for configuration management

- What naming convention will be used to identify products of this project

- What types of product are to be covered

- What types of status are to be used (e.g. 'allocated', 'draft available', 'quality checked').

Once a product has been identified as required, it should receive an identifier from the configuration management method. Sensibly this should coincide with the creation of a draft Product Description.

Among the configuration management planning activities required are those to identify what **baselines** will be required (baselines are explained later in the chapter) and for what purpose, which baselines exist concurrently and which cannot, and when baselines will be taken.

The status of a product should be tracked from the moment the Product Description is created.

CONFIGURATION ITEM ATTRIBUTES

The detail to be kept about the products will depend to some extent on the complexity of the end product, the number of products, the resources available to keep the records and the information demanded by the maintenance and support groups. Below is a list of potential information about a product that should be considered against the needs of the project.

Part Number	A unique configuration identifier allocated by either the Configuration Management software or the Configuration Librarian
Title	The name of the product
Purpose	
Composition	
Format	These five fields are those from a Product Description and contain exactly the same information
Quality Check Method	
Quality Criteria	
Checklist identity	Reference to a checklist which would help check the quality of the product
Provided by	Name of the supplier if from an external source
Current version	Number of this particular version of the product. This is usually linked to a baseline. You may wish to divide this into version and subversion number, for example '3.1'
Category	This can identify the category of product, such as hardware, software, electrical, packing, documentation, etc.
Type	This usually amplifies 'category'. It might define the model, type of hardware, operating product, manual, education material and so on. It might also be used to identify documents as design, or source code
Variant	A product that has the same basic functionality as another product but is different in some small way – an example would be another country's currency symbol
Serial No. or software reference	The serial number of a device or bought-in package
Location	Where the product is physically kept

Status	Current status of the configuration item – you might have your own ideas on the possible entries for this, but the following list may give you some extra ideas:
	Product not defined
	Product Description in progress
	Product Description written
	Product Description approved
	Product ordered
	Product in progress
	Draft version available
	Product in test
	Product under review
	Product approved
	Product accepted
	Product delivered
	Product installed
	Product under change
	(Not all of these need be used, just those that fit your status needs)
Start date of the current status	
Forecast or actual date of the next status change	Date when the next baseline will be taken
Project stage in which it will be developed	
Responsible officer	Who is responsible for production of the product?
Start date of this responsibility	
End date of the responsibility	

Parent	The accepted meaning of this is that if a product has several parts, the product is the 'parent' and the parts 'children'. Another rule is generally that a 'child' can have only one 'parent', even if it is used elsewhere
Child	This is the reverse of the above, showing links to whatever its 'child' component items are
Used in	Apart from the one 'parent', this identifies any other item of which it forms a part
Uses	Links to other items which form part of it, but of which it is not the 'parent'
Change	Cross-references to the issue log entry or entries that affect it
Quality file	Cross-reference to the quality file where information about the quality check of the product is held

The Product Description should be filed in the quality file. If you do this, the full Product Description entries described above may not be needed here. But an alternative is to use software to keep it as part of the configuration management information.

BASELINES

Baselines are moments in a product's evolution when it and all its components have reached an acceptable state, such that they can be 'frozen' and used as a base for the next step. The next step may be to release the product to the customer, or it may be that you have 'frozen' a design and will now construct the products.

Products constantly evolve and are subject to change as a project moves through its life cycle and, later on, in the operational life of the product. A Project Manager will need to know the answer to many questions, such as:

- What is the latest agreed level of specification to which we are working?

- What exact design are we implementing?

- What did we release to site X last January?

In other words, a baseline is a frozen picture of what products and what versions of them constituted a certain situation. A baseline may be defined as a set of known and agreed configuration items under change control from which further progress can be charted. This description indicates that you will baseline only products that represent either the entire product or at least a significant product.

A baseline is created for one of a number of reasons:

- To provide a sound base for future work

- As a point to which you can retreat if development goes wrong

- As an indication of the component and version numbers of a release

- As a bill of material showing the variants released to a specific site

- To copy the products and documentation at the current baseline to all remote sites

- To represent a standard configuration (e.g. Product Description) against which supplies can be obtained (e.g. purchase of personal computers for a group)

- To indicate the state the product must reach before it can be released or upgraded

- As a comparison of one baseline against another in terms of the products contained and their versions

- To transfer configuration items to another library, e.g. from development to production, from the supplier to the customer at the end of the project

- To obtain a report on what products of the baseline are not of status 'X'.

The baseline record itself should be a product, so that it can be controlled in the same way as other products. It is a baseline identifier, date, reason and list of all the products and their version numbers that comprise that baseline. Because of its different format it is often held in a separate file.

STATUS ACCOUNTING AND AUDITING

Configuration status accounting provides a complete statement of the current status and history of the products generated within the project or within a stage. Configuration auditing checks whether the recorded description of products matches their physical representation and whether items have been built to their specification.

CONFIGURATION STATUS ACCOUNTING

The purpose of this is to provide a report on:

- The status of one or all configuration items

- All the events which have impacted those products.

This allows comparison with the plans and provides tracking of changes to products.

In order to provide this information it is necessary for the configuration management method to record all the transactions affecting each configuration item. At the simplest level this means that we can tell the status of each item and version. If we can afford to keep complete records, our library will have broken the specification down into parts, which are linked to design items, which in turn link to constructed components. All approved changes to any one of these will show the linkages and dates of any amendment, plus the baselines incorporating the changes. Our records will show who was responsible and possibly the costs.

For the purpose of status accounting the configuration management method should be able to produce reports on such things as:

- What is the history of development of a particular item?

- How many Requests for Change were approved last month?

- Who is responsible for this item?

- What items in the design baseline have been changed since it was approved?

- On what items have changes been approved but not yet implemented?

CONFIGURATION AUDITING

There are two purposes of configuration auditing. The first is to confirm that the configuration records match reality. In other words, if my configuration records show that we are developing version 3 of a product, I want to be sure that the developer has not moved on to version 5 without my knowing and without any linking documentation to say why versions 4 and 5 have been created. The second purpose is to account for any differences between a delivered product and its original agreed specification. In other words, can the configuration records trace a path from the original specification through any approved changes to what a product looks like now. These audits should verify that:

- All authorised versions of configuration items exist

- Only authorised configuration items exist

- All change records and release records have been properly authorised by project management

- Implemented changes are as authorised.

This is defined as an inspection of the recorded configuration item description and the current representation of that item to ensure that the latter matches its current specification. The inspection also checks that the specification of each item is consistent with that of its parent in the structure. In a sense, it can be regarded as similar to stock control. Does the book description match what we have on the shelf? In addition the audit should ensure that documentation is complete and that project standards have been met.

In engineering establishments, the aim of configuration auditing is to check that, in spite of changes that may have taken place in requirements and design, the items produced conform to the latest agreed specification and that quality review procedures have been performed satisfactorily. Verifying at successive baselines that the item produced at each baseline conforms to the specification produced for it in the previous baseline plus any approved changes does this.

Configuration audits should be done:

- Shortly after implementation of a new configuration management product

- Before and after major changes to the structure of the project's end product

- After disasters such as the loss of records

- On detection of any 'rash' of unauthorised configuration items

- Randomly.

Configuration Audit Checklist

Here is an example checklist for an audit. The following items should be examined:

- Do the configuration records match the physical items?

- Are (randomly tested) approved changes recorded in the Issue Log? Are they linked to the appropriate products? Is their implementation controlled by the configuration management method?

- Does the configuration library accurately reflect the inclusion of any random products? Are there links to relevant Project Issues?

- Are regular configuration audits carried out? Are the results recorded? Have follow-on actions been performed?

- Are (randomly tested) archived and back-up versions of products retained and recorded in the correct manner?

- Are the recorded versions of products used in multiple locations correct?

- Do product names and version numbers meet naming conventions?

- Is configuration library housekeeping carried out in accordance with defined procedures?

- Are staff adequately trained?

- Can baselines be easily and accurately created, recreated and used?

BUILDING A RELEASE PACKAGE

At the end of a project the product that has been developed is released into production. For many installations this may be a simple matter. The product will run operationally in the same environment used for its development, and 'release' is nothing more than 'cutting the tape'.

But there can be many problems concerned with the move of development work over to live operation:

- How do we release details of how to build the product to a sister company on another site?

- How do we ensure that we only release products that have been thoroughly tested as part of the whole product?

- How do we create innumerable copies of the product (like a software house or electrical component manufacturer) and guarantee that they will be identical?

- How can we change an operational product without the risk of it malfunctioning after the change?

- How can we keep a check on which of our customers or sites has what version of the product?

- How do we install a major enhancement of a product?

- If the people who developed the product are not to be the people who install the product, how do they know how to do it?

- Do we issue the complete product for every update or just the changed components?

- Do we issue a complete new operating manual or only the changed pages?

The answer is in release control, another important job for the Configuration Librarian. The tasks for the Configuration Librarian are:

- Identify the products to be included in the release

- Ensure that all the required products have reached a status which allows them to be released into live operation

- Report on any required products that do not have a current approved status

- Build a release package

- List the changes since the previous release and the error reports or requests for change solved by the release

- Distribute the release

- Be able to recreate any baseline (i.e. past release) if a site reports problems on a release

- Know which site has what version and variant of the product.

CONTROL OF RELEASES

Each product release should have a release identifier of the same form as the version number described for a product (i.e. baseline number, issue number) which identifies:

- The level of functionality provided by the release – defined by the baseline number

- The modification status of the release – defined by the issue number

- The release configuration – by reference to the relevant baseline summary.

Revision of release and issue number

The release identifier should be revised:

- When the new release of the product provides changed functionality – the baseline number is incremented up to the next whole number (e.g. 2.1 becomes 3.0)

- When the new release of the product provides fault fixes only – the issue number is incremented by one (e.g. 1.4 becomes 1.5)

- **Optionally** when the new release of the product consolidates many (e.g. 20) minor changes – the baseline number is incremented up to the next whole number.

Release package contents

A release should be accompanied by a release build summary. It should contain:

- The release name and identifier

- The release date

- The person/section/group with responsibility for the release. This will normally be the contact for any installation problems. If not then this information should be added

- A brief description of the release, whether it is a complete or partial release, what has caused the release, what is its purpose, the major benefits over previous releases

- A list of prerequisites for the installation of the release

- A list of all the Project Issues answered by this release

- A bill of material, listing what is contained in the release. This should cover documentation and any procedures

- Assembly steps

- Assembly test steps

- Any customisation steps. If the release can be tailored in any way, this describes the possibilities and lists the steps to be carried out

- Notification of any dates when support for previous releases will cease

- An acknowledgement to be completed and returned by the assembler on successful completion of the assembly.

While current, a baseline cannot be changed. It remains active until it is superseded by the next baseline.

Project Filing

This is a suggested filing system to be used by a project.

There are three major types of file in PRINCE2:

- Management
- Specialist
- Quality.

It is a project decision whether to include the management and quality products within the configuration management method. Even if they are not, a project filing system will still be needed.

MANAGEMENT FILES

These comprise:

- A project file
- A stage file for each stage.

The Project File

This has the following sections:

- Organisation
  The project organisation chart and signed job descriptions.

- Plans
  The Project Plans. This should include any versions developed, not only the one approved as part of the Project Initiation Document. All the various components of each version should be kept (such as Product Breakdown Structures, Product Flow Diagrams) with clear identification of their date, version number and reasoning, such as change of assumptions, scope, resource availability and so on.

  The Project Plan should be updated at least at the end of each stage.

- Business Case
  Versions of the Business Case, updated at each stage end or when Exception Plans are created.

- Risk Log
  Updated details of all identified risks, their status and countermeasures.

- Control
  Copies of Project Initiation and Closure documents.

Stage Files

These have more sections than the project file:

- Organisation
  Stage organisation, details of team members. These should reflect all work assignments, achievements and the Project or Team Manager's assessment of the work performance.

- Plans
  Copies of the Stage Plans, any Team Plans and Exception Plans, updated with actual information as available.

- Control
  Copies of Work Packages, Checkpoint Reports, Highlight Reports, Exception Reports, the End Stage Assessment plus any Mid-Stage Assessments held.

- Daily Log
  A diary of events, problems, questions, answers, informal discussions with Project Board members, and actions for the stage.

- Correspondence
  Copies of management correspondence or other papers associated with the stage.

THE SPECIALIST FILE(S)

This contains all the configuration items of the project, and is the centre of the configuration management activity referred to in the earlier part of this chapter.

There will be a log with identification details of every Configuration Item Record and a reference to its physical location. This method should also cater for sensitive products that must be filed separately.

If an Off-Specification is raised about a product, a copy of the Off-Specification form is filed with the relevant Configuration Item Record in this section of the filing.

Specialist Correspondence

There may also be a need to create this section of the specialist file, where correspondence or external documents cannot be specifically related to one product. The section should have its own log of entries, showing cross-references to the Configuration Item Records concerned.

THE QUALITY FILE

The objective of a Quality File is to permit an audit at any time of the quality of work being done and to confirm adherence to quality standards. There is one Quality File that runs through the whole project and is not divided into stages. It has three major divisions, Product Descriptions, Quality Checks and Project Issues:

Product Descriptions

The master copy of all Product Descriptions. There should be a Product Description for every major product in the project.

Quality Checks

It is useful to head this section with a log giving a number to each check, the type of check or test (e.g. Quality Review), the product and date. This is a quick reference to see or show how many checks have been held in a particular stage and a guide to where the appropriate documentation can be found.

The division of the quality section will depend on the type(s) of check or test being made. The filing for Quality Reviews, for example, should have separate sections for:

- Invitations
- Result notifications
- Action lists.

Project Issues

This should have the Issue Log at the front to facilitate sequential numbering and to record the status and allocation. The subject of Project Issues is covered fully in Chapter 17.

Links

Configuration management links to quality. If you lose control over which versions should be used, or release old versions of components or allow the release of an untested change, the quality of the product will suffer.

There is a very strong link between configuration management and change control. They are inseparable. You can't have one without the other.

Do's and Don'ts

Do relate the complexity of the configuration management method to the needs of the project.

Don't underestimate the importance of configuration management. As was said at the beginning of the chapter, if there is more than yourself working on the project, if there will be more than one version of a product, you need configuration management. Make sure that it's adequate for the job.

If it's a Large Project

The Configuration Librarian role should be part of the Project Support Office, probably using one of the software tools available on the market. If the customer already has a configuration management method in place to look after all products in live operation, the project should use the same method.

If it can be foreseen that there will be many changes during the life of the project, consider whether you should recommend the use of a change authority with its own budget for changes. There is a low limit on the amount of time that Project Board members have to consider changes, and it may be sensible to delegate this, possibly to those performing the Project Assurance roles.

If it's a Small Project

Members of the team can probably do configuration management. I looked at a feasibility study where one of the analysts performed the Configuration Librarian's job. It took about two hours of his time each week. There was a lockable filing cabinet in which the various versions of sections of the report were kept. Team members were responsible for telling the librarian when they wanted to move to a new version. The librarian checked the log and allocated the next version number, having first logged the reason for the change. These reasons had to be documented. Once a fortnight the analyst would take the configuration records round the office and check that there was a match between the records and the version numbers being used.

19 | Product-based Planning

Product-based planning is fundamental to PRINCE2 and I thoroughly recommend it. There are two reasons for this. First, a project delivers products, not activities, so why begin at a lower level? The second reason is about quality. We can measure the quality of a product. The quality of an activity can only be measured by the quality of its outcome (the product).

Product-based planning has three components:

- Product Breakdown Structure
- Product Descriptions
- Product Flow Diagram.

Product Breakdown Structure

Most planning methods begin a plan by thinking of the activities to be undertaken, and listing these in a hierarchical structure called a Work Breakdown Structure (WBS). These activities, however, depend on what products are required to be produced by the project, so the correct start point for a plan is to list the products. In fact, by jumping straight to the lower level of detail of activities, it is possible to miss some vital products and hence vital activities from the plan.

A Product Breakdown Structure is a hierarchy of the products that the plan requires to produce. At the top of the hierarchy is the end product, e.g. a computer system, a new yacht, a department relocated to a new building. This is then broken down into its major constituents at the next level. Each constituent is then broken down into its parts, and this process continues until the planner has reached the level of detail required for the plan.

Let's take an example of a project whose objective is to procure a product. There are many complications that can occur in procurement, but for the sake of an example we shall keep this simple (Figure 19.1).

Product Description

For each identified product, at all levels of the Product Breakdown Structure, a description is produced. Its creation forces the planner to consider if sufficient is known about the product in order to plan its production. It is also the first time that the quality of the product is considered. The quality criteria indicate how much and what type of quality checking will be required.

The purposes of this are, therefore, to provide a guide:

- To the planner on how much effort will be required to create the product
- To the author of the product on what is required
- Against which the finished product can be measured.

These descriptions are a vital checklist to be used at a quality check of the related products.

The description should contain:

- The purpose of the product
- The products from which it is derived
- The composition of the product
- Any standards for format and presentation
- The quality criteria to be applied to the product
- The quality verification method to be used.

The Product Description is given to both the product's creator and those who will verify its quality.

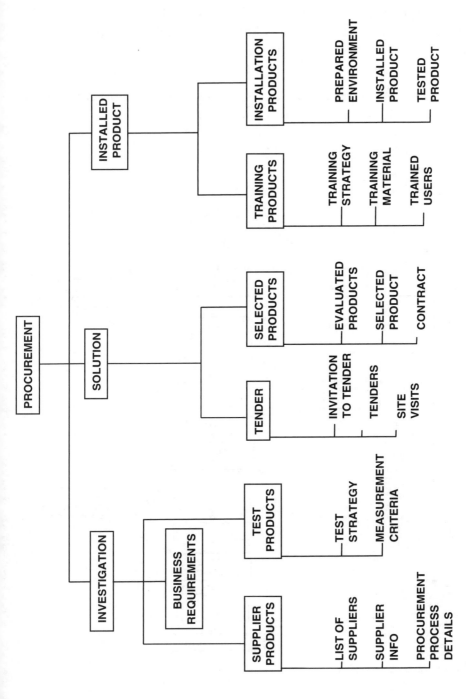

Figure 19.1

Product Flow Diagram

The Product Flow Diagram (PFD) is a diagram showing the sequence in which the products have to be produced and the dependencies between them. It is produced after the Product Breakdown Structure. Figure 19.2 shows a PFD for the procurement example.

A PFD normally needs only two symbols: a rectangle to contain the product and an arrow to show the dependency.

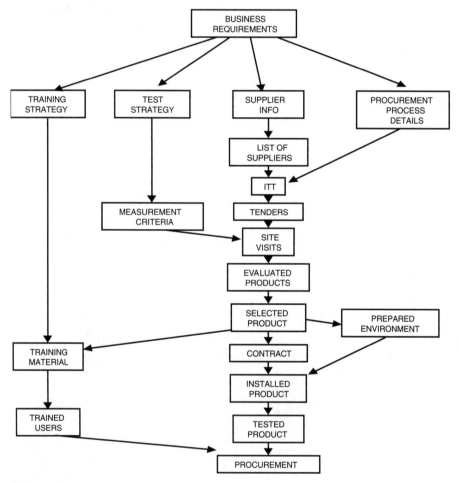

Figure 19.2

External Dependencies

There are times when you may wish to show that the plan is dependent on one or more products over the delivery of which you have no control. To illustrate how we would show such products in our diagrams, let's take the following situation:

> *The lecturer will give you a scenario. Draw a Product Breakdown Structure and a Product Flow Diagram for the project described in the scenario. When you have completed the PBS the lecturer will give you an envelope containing the names of two products for which you then have to create Product Descriptions.*

The PBS and PFD for this statement would look like Figure 19.3.

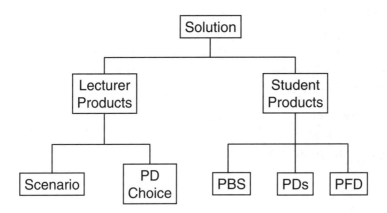

Figure 19.3

Here we can see the PBS is drawn based on the scenario. Once this is done, the PFD can be drawn and the Product Descriptions written – in any order or in parallel. But the Product Descriptions are dependent on receiving the PD choice from the lecturer (Figure 19.4).

The external products, i.e. those over which you have no control, are put in an ellipse to differentiate them from the products over which you have control. If you wish to use the ellipse (or whatever symbol you have chosen) in the PBS to show external products, this is perfectly acceptable.

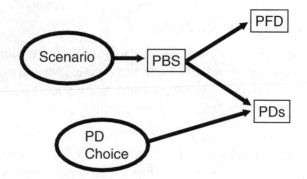

Figure 19.4

Management Products

Another important departure from other methods is the emphasis that, as well as the technical or specialist products of a project, there are always management products. Listing these will remind us that they too take effort to produce and need to be planned as much as the production of technical products.

The management products are much the same for every project. Figures 19.5 and 19.6 show sample Product Breakdown Structures of the management products.

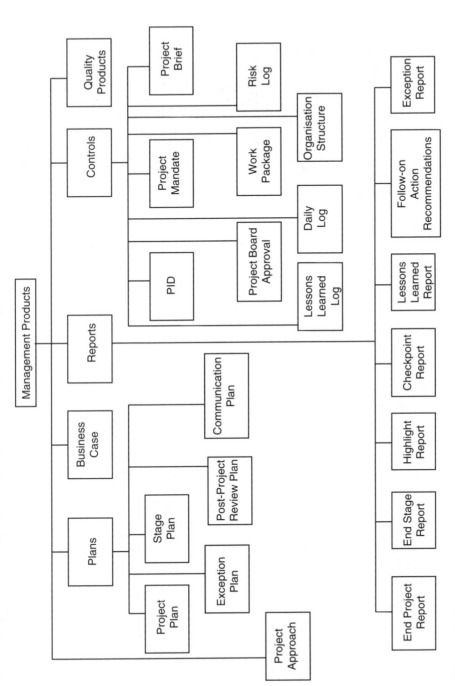

Figure 19.5

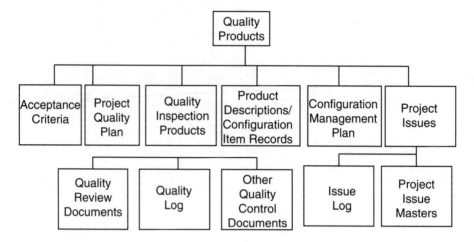

Figure 19.6

20 | Quality Review

This is a team method of checking a product's quality by a review process. The purpose of a Quality Review is to inspect a product for errors in a planned, independent, controlled and documented manner and ensure that any errors found are fixed.

The Quality Review technique is a structured way of reviewing products and products and running a meeting on the review to ensure that all aspects are properly covered. It needs to be used with common sense to avoid the dangers of an overbureaucratic approach but with the intent to follow the procedures laid down (to ensure nothing is missed).

The major aim is to improve product quality. There are several subordinate objectives. These are to:

- Trap errors as early as possible

- Encourage the concept of products as team property rather than belonging to an individual

- Enhance product status data (i.e. not only has the creator declared it finished, but others have confirmed that it is of good quality)

- Monitor the use of standards

- Spread knowledge of the product among those whose own products may interact with it.

Quality Review documentation, when filed in the Quality File, provides, together with the Quality Log, a record that the product was inspected, that any errors found were corrected and that the corrections were themselves checked. Knowing that a product has been checked and declared error free provides a more confident basis to move ahead and use that product as the basis of future work.

People Involved

The interests of parties who should be considered when drawing up the list of attendees are:

- The product author
- Those with Project Assurance responsibilities delegated by the Project Board
- The customer
- Staff who will operate or maintain the finished product
- Other staff whose work will be affected by the product
- Specialists in the relevant product area
- Standards representatives.

Roles at the Quality Review

The roles involved in a Quality Review are (Figure 20.1):

- The Producer, who is the author of the product being reviewed. This role has to ensure that the Reviewers have all the required information in order to perform their job. This means getting a copy of the product from the Configuration Librarian to them during the preparation phase, plus any documents needed to put it in context. Then the Producer has to answer questions about the product during the review until a decision can be reached on whether there is an error or not. Finally the Producer will do most, if not all, of the correcting work. The Producer must not be allowed to be defensive about the product.
- The Chairman. An open, objective attitude is needed. The Chairman has the following required attributes:

Figure 20.1

- Sufficient authority to control the review

- Understands the Quality Review process thoroughly

- Chairmanship experience.

The Chairman is responsible for ensuring that the Quality Review is properly organised and that it runs smoothly during all of its phases.

For the preparation phase this includes checking that administrative procedures have been carried out and that the right people have been invited. This needs consultation with any appointed Project Assurance roles and reference to the Stage Plan.

- The Reviewers, who must be competent to assess the product from their particular viewpoints.

- A Scribe – someone to note down the agreed actions. Very often this role is taken by someone from Project Support.

It must be remembered that these are roles. They must all be present at a Quality Review, but a person may take on more than one role.

Phases

There are three distinct phases within the Quality Review procedure: preparation, review and follow-up.

PHASE 1 – PREPARATION

See Figure 20.2.

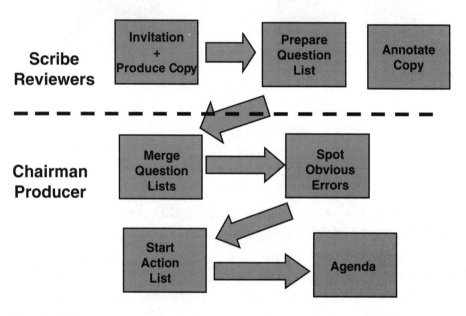

Figure 20.2

The objective of this phase is to examine the product under review and to create a list of questions (or possible errors) for the review.

The Chairman checks with the Producer that the product will be ready on time. If not, the Project Manager is advised. This will lead to an update of the Stage Plan. The Chairman ensures that the team of Reviewers is agreed, that they will all be available and that the venue has been arranged.

An invitation is sent out, giving the time and place for the review with copies of the product, the relevant Product Description and any checklist available. This should be done with sufficient time before the review to allow the Reviewers time to examine the product and to provide a Question List to the producer.

Each Reviewer will study the product and supporting documents (including the quality criteria in the Product Description), annotate the product, and complete a Question List.

A copy of the Question Lists will, wherever possible, be sent to the Producer before the review. The Producer and Chairman should review these to allow the Chairman to set up an agenda, prioritise the questions and roughly allocate time to each point. To save time at the review, the Producer can acknowledge questions that identify agreed errors.

PHASE 2 – REVIEW

The objective of the review is to agree a list of any actions needed to correct or complete the product. The Chairman and the Producer do not have to reconcile these actions at the meeting – it is sufficient for the Chairman and Reviewers to agree that a particular area needs correction or at least re-examination. Provided that the action is logged the Reviewers have an opportunity in the next phase to confirm that action has been taken.

The Chairman opens the meeting and introduces those present if necessary. Timing (suggested maximum of two hours) is announced.

The Producer then 'walks through' the questions in detail. The Reviewers' Question Lists already sent to the Producer will determine this. If it is found that any part is understood and accepted, there is no point in walking through it.

The Chairman controls the discussion during the review, ensuring that no arguments or solutions are discussed (other than obvious and immediately accepted solutions!). The Scribe notes actions on an Action List. No other minutes are taken of the review.

At the conclusion of the walk-through, the Chairman asks the Scribe to read back the actions and determines responsibility for correction of any points. A target date is set for each action and the initials of the Reviewer(s) who will sign off each corrective action as it is completed and found acceptable are recorded on the Action List by the Scribe.

The Chairman, after seeking the Reviewers' and Producer's opinions, will decide on the outcome of the review. There can be one of three outcomes:

- The product is error free

- The product will be acceptable on completion of the actions noted

- There is so much corrective work to be done that the entire product needs to be re-reviewed.

In the latter case, the Chairman will advise the Project Manager so that the Stage Plan can be updated. The Quality Log is updated. A result notification will be completed and the documents attached. These forms will be filed in the Quality File.

The Reviewers' Question Lists, copies of the product (probably containing the Reviewer's annotations) and any other relevant documentation is collected by the Chairman and passed to the Producer to assist in the follow-up.

PHASE 3 – FOLLOW-UP

The objective of the follow-up phase is to ensure that all actions identified on the Action List are dealt with (Figure 20.3).

The Producer takes the Action List away from the review and evaluates, discusses, and corrects, if necessary, all the errors.

When an error has been fixed, the Producer will obtain sign-off from whoever is nominated on the Action List. This person may be the Reviewer who raised the query initially, but other Reviewers have the option of checking the correction.

QUALITY REVIEW FOLLOW-UP

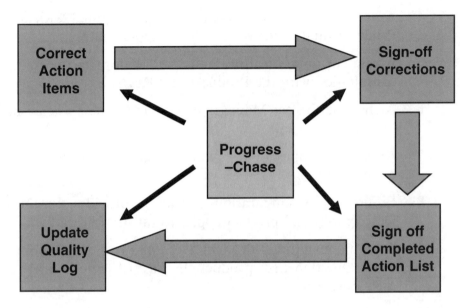

Figure 20.3

When all errors have been reconciled and sign-off obtained, the Chairman will confirm that the product is complete and sign off the Action List. The documents will be filed in the Quality File and the Stage Plan updated.

Quality Review Responsibilities

CHAIRMAN'S RESPONSIBILITIES

Preparation Phase

1. Check with the Producer that the product is ready for review.

2. If not, update the Stage Plan, e.g. a revised completion date.

3. Consult with the Producer and those performing Project Assurance roles to confirm appropriate Reviewers.

4. Agree the amount of preparation time required with the Producer (and Reviewers, if this is appropriate).

5. Arrange a time, location and duration for the review in consultation with the Producer and Reviewers.

6. Advise the Project Manager if there is to be any delay in holding the review.

7. Arrange for copies of any relevant checklist or standard to be provided.

8. Ensure the Configuration Librarian provides Product Descriptions and product copies for all Reviewers.

9. Send an invitation, Product Description, product copy, blank Question List, product checklist (if there is one) to each Reviewer.

10. Send a copy of the invitation to the Producer.

11. Decide if a short overview presentation of the product to the Reviewers is required as part of the preparation, and arrange it if it is.

12. Arrange with the Reviewers for collection of their Question Lists prior to the review.

13. Create an agenda for the review from the Question Lists in consultation with the Producer. Agree any obvious errors in the product with the Producer. Prioritise the questions and roughly allocate time.

14. Confirm attendance with each Reviewer shortly before the review. If a Reviewer cannot attend, ensure that the Reviewer's Question List is made out and submitted. If too many Reviewers cannot attend, reschedule the review and inform the Project Manager of the delay.

15. If necessary, rehearse the review with the Producer.

Review

1. Provide a copy of the agenda to all attendees.

2. Open the review, stating objectives and apologising for any non-attendees.

3. Decide whether the Reviewers present and the Question Lists from those unable to attend are adequate to review the product. If not, the review should be stopped, rescheduled and the Project Manager advised.

4. Identify any errors in the product already agreed by the Producer and ensure that these are documented on the Action List.

5. Step through the agenda, with the appropriate Reviewer enlarging where necessary on the question.

6. Allow reasonable discussion on each question between Producer and Reviewers to decide if action is required.

7. Ensure that the Scribe documents any agreed actions required on an Action List.

8. Prevent any discussion of possible solutions or matters of style.

9. Ensure that Reviewers are given a chance to voice their comments.

10. Where agreement cannot be reached on a point in a reasonable timeframe, declare it an action point and note the Reviewer(s) concerned.

11. Where necessary, decide on the premature close of the review in the light of the comments made.

12. If faults are identified in products not under review, ensure that a Project Issue is raised and sent to the Configuration Librarian.

13. Collect any annotated products detailing minor or typographical errors.

14. Read back the Action List and obtain confirmation from the Producer and Reviewers that it is complete and correct.

15. Identify who is to be involved in working on each action item. Obtain a target date for completion of the work.

16. Agree with the Reviewers who is to approve the work done on each action item and note this on the Action List.

17. Pass the Action List and all copies of the annotated product to the Producer. Lodge a copy of the Action List in the Quality File.

18. Decide with the Reviewers what the status of the review is. It can be:

    • Complete with no errors discovered

    • Complete with some rework required

    • In need of rework and another review.

19. If the review is incomplete, recommend a course of action to the Project Manager. There are five possible courses of action. The last two of these are not recommended:

    • The product should be reworked prior to another review

    • The review should be reconvened to finish with no interim need for rework

    • The review should be reconvened without rework with a different set of Reviewers

    • The review should be declared complete, the errors found so far corrected and the rest of the product accepted as is

    • The review should be abandoned and the product used as is, i.e. none of the errors corrected, but noted in a Project Issue.

Follow-up

1. Monitor the correction of errors and sign off the Action List when all corrections have been approved.

2. If an action cannot be taken within the time agreed, the Chairman and Producer may decide to transfer it to a Project Issue as a possible error. This requires the agreement of the Project Manager. The Action List is updated with the Project Issue log number and those waiting to sign off the action item informed.

3. On completion and sign-off of all action items, sign off the Action List as complete and file it in the Quality File with copies to all Reviewers. Update the Quality Log.

4. Supervise the passage of the error-free product to the Configuration Librarian.

PRODUCER'S RESPONSIBILITIES

Preparation

1. Ask the Project Manager to nominate a Chairman if none is identified in the Stage Plan.

2. Confirm with the Chairman that the product is ready for review. This should occur several days prior to the planned review date to allow for preparation time.

3. Confirm the attendees with the Chairman and those holding Project Assurance responsibilities.

4. Agree with the Chairman and Reviewers the length of preparation time needed and review location.

5. Assess the Question Lists from the Reviewers, identifying any errors in the product that can be agreed without further discussion.

6. Agree the agenda with the Chairman in the light of the Question Lists.

Review

1. Answer any questions about the product.

2. Offer an opinion to the Chairman on whether a question has highlighted an error in the product.

3. If the review is judged to be complete, collect from the Chairman the Action List and any annotated copies of the product from the Reviewers.

Follow-up

1. Resolve all allocated action items.

2. Obtain sign-off for each action item from the nominated Reviewers.

3. If an action item cannot be resolved within a reasonable timeframe, then the Chairman and Producer may decide to transfer it to a Project Issue. An alternative is to agree new target dates.

4. Pass the Action List to the Chairman on resolution of all the action items.

REVIEWER'S RESPONSIBILITIES

Preparation

1. Consult the Product Description and any pertinent checklists and standards against which the product should be judged.

2. Allow sufficient time to prepare for the review.

3. Consult any necessary source documents from which the product is derived.

4. Annotate any spelling or typographical mistakes on the product copy, but do not add these to the Question List.

5. Check the product for completeness, defects, ambiguities, inconsistencies, lack of clarity or deviations from standards. Note any such items on the Question List.

6. Forward the Question List to the Chairman in advance of the review. If possible, this should be done early enough to give the Producer time to digest the points and prepare an agenda with the Chairman.

7. Forward a Question List and the annotated product copy to the Chairman if unable to attend the review.

Review

1. Ensure that the points noted on the Question List are raised at the review.

2. Restrict comments to faults in the product under review.

3. Avoid attempting to redesign the product.

4. Avoid 'improvement' comments if the product meets requirements and standards.

5. Verify and approve the Action List as complete and correct when read back by the Chairman.

6. Agree to assist in the resolution of any action items if requested by the Chairman.

7. Request to check and sign off any action items either raised personally or which impact on the Reviewer's area of expertise or interest.

Follow-up

1. Work with the Producer to resolve any allocated action item.

2. Check and sign off those action items where allocated as Reviewer.

Formal and Informal Reviews

Quality Reviews can be either formal (i.e. a scheduled meeting conducted as described above) or informal (i.e. a 'get-together' between two people to informally walk through a product). A variation on a formal review is to have the Reviewers forward their Action Lists, but only the Chairman and the Producer do the actual review.

Informal Quality Reviews will follow a similar format to the Formal Quality Review – the paperwork emerging from both meetings is similar. The main difference will be the informality of the proceedings during the three phases and the overall time required.

For informal Quality Reviews two people can be given the task of checking each other's work on an ongoing basis. Alternatively an experienced person can be asked to regularly hold reviews of an inexperienced person's work as it develops.

Factors in deciding whether a formal or informal review is needed are:

- The importance of the product
- Whether it is a final deliverable
- Whether it is the source for a number of other products
- The author's experience
- Who the product's consumer is
- Whether it is a review of a partial document.

21	**Project Management Team Roles**

This chapter provides a description for each role in the project management structure. These can be used as the basis for discussion of an individual's job and tailored to suit the project's circumstances. The tailored role description becomes that person's job description for the project. Two copies of an agreed job description should be signed by the individual, one for retention by the individual, the other to be filed in the project file.

Project Board

GENERAL

The Project Board is appointed by corporate/programme management to provide overall direction and management of the project. The Project Board is accountable for the success of the project, and has responsibility and authority for the project within the limits set by corporate/programme management.

The Project Board is the project's 'voice' to the outside world and is responsible for any publicity or other dissemination of information about the project.

SPECIFIC RESPONSIBILITY

The Project Board approves all major plans and authorises any major deviation from agreed Stage Plans. It is the authority that signs off the completion of each stage as well as authorises the start of the next stage. It ensures that required resources are committed and arbitrates on any conflicts within the project or negotiates a solution to any problems between the project and external bodies. In addition, it approves the appointment and responsibility of the Project Manager and any delegation of its Project Assurance responsibilities.

The Project Board has the following responsibility. It is a general list and will need tailoring for a specific project.

At the beginning of the project:

- Assurance that the PID complies with relevant customer standards and policies, plus any associated contract with the supplier
- Agreement with the Project Manager on that person's responsibility and objectives
- Confirmation with corporate/programme management of project tolerances
- Specification of external constraints on the project such as quality assurance
- Approval of an accurate and satisfactory Project Initiation Document
- Delegation of any Project Assurance roles
- Commitment of project resources required by the next Stage Plan.

As the project progresses:

- Provision of overall guidance and direction to the project, ensuring it remains within any specified constraints
- Review of each completed stage and approval of progress to the next
- Review and approval of Stage Plans and any Exception Plans
- 'Ownership' of one or more of the identified project risks as allocated at plan approval time, i.e. the responsibility to monitor the risk and advise the Project Manager of any

change in its status and to take action, if appropriate, to ameliorate the risk

- Approval of changes
- Compliance with corporate/programme management directives.

At the end of the project:

- Assurance that all products have been delivered satisfactorily
- Assurance that all acceptance criteria have been met
- Approval of the End Project Report
- Approval of the Lessons Learned Report and the passage of this to the appropriate standards group to ensure action
- Decisions on the recommendations for follow-on actions and the passage of these to the appropriate authorities
- Arrangements, where appropriate, for a post-project review
- Project closure notification to corporate/programme management.

The Project Board is ultimately responsible for the assurance of the project, that it remains on course to deliver the desired outcome of the required quality to meet the Business Case defined in the project contract. According to the size, complexity and risk of the project, the Project Board may decide to delegate some of these Project Assurance responsibilities. Later in this chapter Project Assurance is defined in more detail.

One Project Board responsibility that should receive careful consideration is that of approving and funding changes. Chapter 17 should be read before finalising this responsibility of approving and funding changes.

Responsibilities of specific members of the Project Board are described in the respective sections below.

Executive

GENERAL

The Executive is ultimately responsible for the project, supported by the Senior User and Senior Supplier. The Executive has to ensure that the project is value for money, ensuring a cost-conscious approach to the project, balancing the demands of business, user and supplier.

Throughout the project the Executive 'owns' the Business Case.

SPECIFIC RESPONSIBILITY

- Ensure that a tolerance is set for the project by corporate/ programme management in the Project Mandate

- Authorise customer expenditure and set stage tolerances

- Brief corporate/programme management about project progress

- Organise and chair Project Board meetings

- Recommend future action on the project to corporate/programme management if the project tolerance is exceeded

- Approve the End Project Report and Lessons Learned Report

- Approve the sending of the notification of project closure to corporate/programme management.

The Executive is responsible for overall business assurance of the project, i.e. that it remains on target to deliver products that will achieve the expected business benefits, and the project will complete within its agreed tolerances for budget and schedule. Business assurance covers:

- Validation and monitoring of the Business Case against external events and against project progress

- Keeping the project in line with customer strategies

- Monitoring project finance on behalf of the customer

- Monitoring the business risks to ensure that these are kept under control

- Monitoring any supplier and contractor payments

- Monitoring changes to the Project Plan to see if there is any impact on the needs of the business or the project Business Case

- Assessing the impact of potential changes on the Business Case and Project Plan

- Constraining user and supplier excesses

- Informing the project of any changes caused by a programme of which the project is part (this responsibility may be transferred if there is other programme representation on the project management team)

- Monitoring stage and project progress against the agreed tolerance.

If the project warrants it, the Executive may delegate some responsibility for the above business assurance functions.

Senior User

GENERAL

The Senior User is responsible for the specification of the needs of all those who will use the final product(s), user liaison with the project team and for monitoring that the solution will meet those needs within the constraints of the Business Case.

The role represents the interests of all those who will use the final product(s) of the project, those for whom the product will achieve an objective, or those who will use the product to deliver benefits. The Senior User role commits user resources and monitors products against requirements. This role may require more than one person to cover all the user interests. For the sake of effectiveness the role should not be split between too many people.

SPECIFIC RESPONSIBILITY

- Ensure the desired outcome of the project is specified
- Make sure that progress towards the outcome required by the users remains consistent from the user perspective
- Promote and maintain focus on the desired project outcome
- Ensure that any user resources required for the project are made available
- Approve Product Descriptions for those products that act as inputs or outputs (interim or final) from the supplier function, or will affect them directly and ensure that the products are signed off once completed
- Prioritise and contribute user opinions to Project Board decisions on whether to implement recommendations on proposed changes
- Resolve user requirements and priority conflicts
- Provide the user view on recommended follow-up actions
- Brief and advise user management on all matters concerning the project.

The assurance responsibilities of the Senior User are that:

- Specification of the user's needs is accurate, complete and unambiguous
- Development of the solution at all stages is monitored to ensure that it will meet the user's needs and is progressing towards that target
- Impact of potential changes is evaluated from the user point of view
- Risks to the users are constantly monitored

- Testing of the product at all stages has the appropriate user representation

- Quality control procedures are used correctly to ensure products meet user requirements

- User liaison is functioning effectively.

Where the project's size, complexity or importance warrants it, the Senior User may delegate the responsibility and authority for some of the assurance responsibilities.

Senior Supplier

GENERAL

Represents the interests of those designing, developing, facilitating, procuring, implementing, operating and maintaining the project products. The Senior Supplier role must have the authority to commit or acquire supplier resources required.

If necessary, more than one person may be required to represent the suppliers.

SPECIFIC RESPONSIBILITY

- Agree objectives for specialist activities

- Make sure that progress towards the outcome remains consistent from the supplier perspective

- Promote and maintain focus on the desired project outcome from the point of view of supplier management

- Ensure that the supplier resources required for the project are made available

- Approve Product Descriptions for specialist products

- Contribute supplier opinions to Project Board decisions on whether to implement recommendations on proposed changes

- Resolve supplier requirements and priority conflicts

- Arbitrate on, and ensure resolution of, any specialist priority or resource conflicts

- Brief non-technical management on specialist aspects of the project.

The Senior Supplier is responsible for the specialist assurance of the project. The specialist Project Assurance role responsibilities are to:

- Advise on the selection of technical strategy, design and methods

- Ensure that any specialist and operating standards defined for the project are met and used to good effect

- Monitor potential changes and their impact on the correctness, completeness and assurance of products against their Product Description from a technical perspective

- Monitor any risks in the specialist and production aspects of the project

- Ensure quality control procedures are used correctly so that products adhere to technical requirements.

If warranted, some of these Project Assurance responsibilities may be delegated.

Project Manager

GENERAL

The Project Manager has the authority to run the project on a day-to-day basis on behalf of the Project Board within the constraints laid down by the board. In a customer/supplier environment the Project Manager will normally come from the customer organisation.

RESPONSIBILITY

The Project Manager's prime responsibility is to ensure that the project produces the required products, to the required standard of quality and within the specified constraints of time and cost. The Project Manager is also responsible for the project producing a result that is capable of achieving the benefits defined in the Business Case.

SPECIFIC RESPONSIBILITIES

- Manage the production of the required products
- Direct and motivate the project team
- Plan and monitor the project
- Agree any delegation and use of Project Assurance roles required by the Project Board
- Produce the project contract
- Prepare Project, Stage and, if necessary, Exception Plans in conjunction with Team Managers, and appointed Project Assurance roles, and obtain Project Board agreement to the plans
- Manage risks, including the development of contingency plans
- Liaise with programme management if the project is part of a programme
- Liaise with programme management or related projects to ensure that work is neither overlooked nor duplicated
- Take responsibility for overall progress and use of resources, and initiate corrective action where necessary
- Be responsible for change control and any required configuration management
- Report to the Project Board through Highlight Reports and end stage assessments
- Liaise with the Project Board or its appointed Project Assurance roles to assure the overall direction and Project Assurance of the project

- Agree technical and quality strategy with appropriate members of the Project Board

- Keep a Lessons Learned Log throughout the project

- Prepare the Lessons Learned Report from the Lessons Learned Log at the end of the project

- Prepare any follow-on action recommendations required

- Prepare the End Project Report

- Identify and obtain any support and advice required for the management, planning and control of the project

- Be responsible for project administration

- Liaise with any suppliers or account managers.

Team Manager

GENERAL

The allocation of this role to one or more people is optional. Where the project does not warrant the use of a Team Manager, the Project Manager takes the role.

The Project Manager may find that it is beneficial to delegate the authority and responsibility for planning the creation of certain products and managing a team of technicians to produce those products. There are many reasons why it may be decided to employ this role. Some of these are the size of the project, the particular specialist skills or knowledge needed for certain products, geographical location of some team members, and the preferences of the Project Board.

The Team Manager's prime responsibility is to ensure production of those products defined by the Project Manager to an appropriate quality, in a timescale and at a cost acceptable to the Project Board. The Team Manager reports to and takes direction from the Project Manager.

The use of this role should be discussed by the Project Manager with the Project Board and, if the role is required, planned at the outset of the project. This is discussed in the 'Starting Up a Project' and 'Initiating a Project' processes.

SPECIFIC GOALS

- Prepare plans for the team's work and agree these with the Project Manager

- Receive authorisation from the Project Manager to create products (Work Package)

- Manage the team

- Direct, motivate, plan and monitor the team work

- Identify and advise the Project Manager of any risks associated with a Work Package

- Ensure that such risks are entered on the Risk Log

- Manage specific risks as directed by the Project Manager

- Take responsibility for the progress of the team's work and use of team resources, and initiate corrective action where necessary within the constraints and tolerances laid down by the Project Manager

- Advise the Project Manager of any deviations from the plan, recommend corrective action, and help prepare any appropriate Exception Plans

- Pass products that have been completed and approved in line with the agreed Work Package requirements back to the Project Manager

- Ensure all Project Issues are properly reported to the person maintaining the Issue Log

- Ensure the evaluation of Project Issues that arise within the team's work and recommend action to the Project Manager

- Liaise with any Project Assurance roles

- Attend any stage assessments as directed by the Project Manager

- Arrange and lead team checkpoints

- Ensure that quality controls of the team's work are planned and performed correctly

- Maintain, or ensure the maintenance of team files.

Project Assurance

GENERAL

The Project Board members do not work full time on the project; therefore they place a great deal of reliance on the Project Manager. Although they receive regular reports from the Project Manager, there may always be the questions at the back of their minds, 'Are things really going as well as we are being told?', 'Are any problems being hidden from us?', 'Is the solution going to be what we want?', 'Are we suddenly going to find that the project is over budget or late?' There are other questions. The supplier may have a quality assurance function charged with the responsibility to check that all projects are adhering to a quality system that is being used.

All of these points mean that there is a need in the project organisation for an independent monitoring of all aspects of the project's performance and products. This is the Project Assurance function.

To cater for a small project, we start by identifying these Project Assurance functions as part of the role of each Project Board member. According to the needs and desires of the Project Board, any of these Project Assurance responsibilities can be delegated, as long as the recipients are independent of the Project Manager. Any appointed Project Assurance jobs assure the project on behalf of one or more members of the Project Board.

It is not mandatory that all Project Assurance roles be delegated. Each of the Project Assurance roles that are delegated may be assigned to one individual or shared. The Project Board decides when a Project Assurance role needs to be delegated. It may be for the entire project or only part of it. The person or persons filling a Project Assurance role may be changed during the project at the request of the Project Board. Any use of Project Assurance roles needs to be planned during the initiation stage, otherwise resource usage and costs for Project Assurance could easily get out of control.

There is no stipulation on how many Project Assurance roles there must be. Each Project Board role has Project Assurance responsibility. Again, each project should determine what support, if any, each Project Board role needs to achieve this Project Assurance.

For example, an international standards group, such as ISO, may certificate the supplier's work standards. A requirement of the certification is that there will be some form of quality assurance function that is required to monitor the supplier's work. The quality assurance could include verification by an external party that the Project Board is performing its functions correctly. Some of the Senior Supplier's Project Assurance responsibilities may be delegated to this function. Note that they would only be delegated. The Project Board member retains accountability. Any delegation should be documented.

Project Assurance covers all interests of a project, including all business, user and supplier.

Project Assurance has to be independent of the Project Manager; therefore the Project Board cannot delegate any of its Project Assurance responsibility to the Project Manager.

SPECIFIC RESPONSIBILITY

The implementation of the Project Assurance responsibility needs to answer the question 'What is to be assured?' A list of possibilities would include:

- Maintenance of thorough liaison throughout the project between the supplier and the customer
- Customer needs and expectations are being met or managed

- Risks are being controlled
- Assurance of adherence to the Business Case
- Constant reassessment of the value-for-money solution
- Fit with the overall programme or company strategy
- The right people are involved
- An acceptable solution is developed
- The project remains viable
- The scope of the project is not 'creeping up' unnoticed
- Focus on the business need is maintained
- Internal and external communications are working
- Applicable standards are being used
- Any legislative constraints are being observed
- The needs of specialist interests, e.g. security, are being observed
- Adherence to quality assurance standards.

It is not enough to believe that standards will be obeyed. It is not enough to ensure that a project is well set up and justified at the outset. All the aspects listed above need to be checked throughout the project as part of ensuring that it remains consistent with and continues to meet a business need and that no change to the external environment affects the validity of the project.

Project Support

GENERAL

The provision of any Project Support on a formal basis is optional. It is driven by the needs of the individual project and Project Manager. Project Support could be in the form of advice on project management tools and administrative services, such as filing, the collection of actual data, to one or more related projects. Where it is set up as an official body, Project Support can act as a repository for lessons learned, and a central source of expertise in specialist support tools.

One support function that must be considered is that of configuration management. Depending on the project size and environment, there may be a need to formalise this, and it quickly becomes a task with which the Project Manager cannot cope without support. See Chapter 18 for details of the work.

MAIN TASKS
The following is a suggested list of tasks.

Administration
- Administer change control
- Set up and maintain project files
- Establish document control procedures
- Compile, copy and distribute all project management products
- Collect actual data and forecasts
- Update plans
- Administer the Quality Review process
- Administer Project Board meetings
- Assist with the compilation of reports.

Advice
- Specialist knowledge (e.g. estimating, management of risk)
- Specialist tool expertise (e.g. planning and control tools, risk analysis)
- Specialist techniques
- Standards.

Appendix 1 Product Descriptions

The following appendix contains suggested Product Descriptions for the PRINCE2 management and quality products. Care should be taken to scrutinise them and tune them to any site or project's specific needs.

Title
Acceptance Criteria

Purpose
A definition in measurable terms of those aspects of the final product that it must demonstrate for the product to be acceptable to the customer and staff who will be affected by the product.

Composition
Criteria suitable for the product, such as:

- Target dates
- Major functions
- Performance levels
- Capacity
- Accuracy
- Appearance
- Availability
- Reliability
- Development cost
- Running costs
- Maintenance
- Security
- Ease of use
- Timings
- Personnel level required to use/operate the product.

Form(at)

This forms part of the Project Brief. It is a list of acceptance criteria, measurements, dates by when each criterion should be met, including any interim measurements and dates.

Derivation

- Background information
- Project Mandate
- Project Brief
- Senior User.

Quality Criteria

- All criteria are measurable
- Each criterion is individually realistic
- The criteria as a group are realistic, e.g. high quality, early delivery and low cost may not go together.

Quality Method

Formal Quality Review between Project Manager and those with Project Assurance responsibility.

Title

Business Case

Purpose

To document the reasons and justification for undertaking a project, based on the estimated cost of development and the anticipated business benefits to be gained. The Project Board will monitor the ongoing viability of the project against the Business Case.

The Business Case may include legal or legislative reasons why the project is needed.

Composition

- Business reasons for undertaking the project
- Business benefits to be gained from development of the product
- Options considered
- Development cost and timescale
- Investment Appraisal
- Major risks.

(These may refer to the overall Business Case if it is part of a programme.)

Form(at)

The Business Case forms part of the Project Initiation Document. Document to standard site practice with the composition shown above.

Derivation

Information for the Business Case is derived from:

- Project Mandate/Project Brief (reasons)
- Project Plan (costs)
- The customer.

Quality Criteria

- Can the benefits be justified?
- Do the cost and timescale match those in the Project Plan?
- Are the reasons for the project consistent with corporate or programme strategy?

Quality Method

Quality Review with the Executive and anyone appointed to business assurance.

Title
Checkpoint Report

Purpose
To report at a frequency defined in the Work Package the progress and status of work for a team.

Composition
- Date of the checkpoint
- Period covered by the report
- Report on any follow-up action from previous reports
- Products completed during the period
- Quality work carried out during the period
- Products to be completed during the next period
- Risk assessment
- Other actual or potential problems or deviations from plan.

Form(at)
According to the agreement between Project Manager and Team Manager, the report may be verbal or written. It should contain the information given above, plus any extra data requested by the Project Manager.

Derivation
- Team Plan actuals and forecasts
- Risk Log
- Team member reports.

Quality Criteria

- Every team member's work covered

- Includes an update on any unresolved problems from the previous report

- Accurately reflects the Team Plan situation

- Reflects any significant change to the Risk Log

- Reflects any change in a team member's work that has an impact on others.

Quality Method

Informal check by Team Manager and those with Project Assurance responsibility.

Title
Communication Plan

Purpose
The Communication Plan identifies all parties who require information from the project and those from whom the project requires information. The plan defines what information is needed and when it should be supplied.

Composition
- Interested parties (such as user groups, suppliers, stakeholders, quality assurance, internal audit)
- Information required by each identified party
- Identity of the information provider
- Frequency of communication
- Method of communication.

Form(at)
To the defined site standard for reports with the above content.

Derivation
- The Project Board
- The Project Brief
- The Project Initiation Document
- The Project Quality Plan
- The Project Approach.

Quality Criteria

- Have all the listed derivation sources been checked?

- Has the timing, content and method been agreed?

- Has a common standard been agreed?

- Has time for the communications been allowed for in the Stage Plans?

Quality Method

Informal Quality Review between Project Manager and those identified in the Communication Plan.

Title
Configuration Item Record.

Purpose
A record of the information required about a product's status.

Composition

- The project identifier
- Type of product
- Product identifier
- Latest version number
- Product Description
- A description of the life cycle steps appropriate to the product
- 'Owner' of the product
- Person working on the product
- Date allocated
- Library or location where the product is kept
- Source – for example, in-house, or purchased from a third party company
- Links to related products
- Status
- Copyholders and potential users
- Cross-reference to the Project Issue(s) that caused the change to this product
- Cross-references to relevant correspondence.

Derivation

- Product Breakdown Structure
- Stage and Team Plans
- Work Package
- Quality Log
- Change control.

Quality Criteria

- Does it reflect the status of the product accurately?
- Are all Configuration Item Records kept together in a secure location?
- Does the version number match the actual product?
- Is the copyholder information correct?
- Do the copies held by the copyholders match the version number?

Title

Configuration Management Plan

Purpose

To identify how and by whom the project's products will be controlled and protected.

Composition

This plan forms part of the Project Quality Plan. It consists of:

- An explanation of the purpose of configuration management
- A description of (or reference to) the configuration management method to be used. Any variance from corporate or programme standards should be highlighted together with a justification for the variance
- Reference to any other configuration management systems with which links will be necessary
- Identification of the Configuration Librarian
- Identification of the products, levels of product, or classes of product that will be controlled under configuration management
- A plan of what libraries and files will be used to hold products
- Confirmation that the relevant project and next stage files have been set up.

Derivation

Details of the plan might come from:

- The customer's quality management system (QMS)
- The supplier's QMS

- Specific needs of the project's products and environment

- The project organisation structure

- Any configuration management software in use or mandated by the customer.

Quality Criteria

- Responsibilities are clear and understood by both customer and supplier

- The key identifier for project products is defined

- The method and circumstances of version control is clear

- The plan provides the Project Manager with all the product information required

- An explanation of the purpose of configuration management

- A description of (or reference to) the configuration management method to be used. Any variance from corporate or programme standards should be highlighted together with a justification for the variance

- Reference to any other configuration management systems with which links will be necessary

- Identification of the Configuration Librarian

- Identification of the products, levels of product, or classes of product that will be controlled under configuration management

- A plan of what libraries and files will be used to hold products

- Confirmation that the relevant project and next stage files have been set up.

Title

Daily Log

Purpose

To record required actions or significant events not caught by other PRINCE2 documents. It acts as the Project Manager's project diary.

Composition

- Project title
- Date of record
- Action or comment
- Person responsible
- Target date
- Result.

Derivation

- Risk Log
- Stage Plan
- Checkpoint Reports
- Quality Log
- Conversations and observations.

Quality Criteria

- Entries are understandable at a later date
- Anything of a permanent nature is transferred to the appropriate record, e.g. Project Issue
- Date, person responsible and target date are always filled in.

Title

End Project Report

Purpose

The report is the Project Manager's report to the Project Board (which may pass it on to corporate or programme management) on how the project has performed against the objectives stated in its Project Initiation Document and revised during the project. It should cover comparisons with the original targets, planned cost, schedule and tolerances, the revised Business Case and final version of the Project Plan.

Composition

- Assessment of the achievement of the project's objectives
- Performance against the planned (and revised) target times and costs
- The effect on the original Project Plan and Business Case of any changes which were approved
- Final statistics on change issues received during the project and the total impact (time, money, benefits, for example) of any approved changes
- Statistics for all quality work carried out
- Post-Project Review date and plan.

Form(at)

To the defined site standard for reports with the above content plus any extra information requested by the Project Board.

Derivation

- The final Project Plan with actuals
- The Project Initiation Document
- Issue Log.

Quality Criteria

- Does the report describe the impact of any approved changes on the original intentions stated in the Project Initiation Document?
- Does the report cover all the benefits that can be assessed at this time?
- Does the quality work done during the project meet the quality expectations of the customer?

Quality Method

Formal Quality Review between Project Manager and those with Project Assurance responsibility.

Title

End Stage Report

Purpose

The purpose of the End Stage Report is to report on a stage that has just completed, the overall project situation and sufficient information to ask for a Project Board decision on the next step to take with the project.

The Project Board use the information in the End Stage Report to approve the next Stage Plan, amend the project scope, ask for a revised next Stage Plan, or stop the project.

Composition

- Current Stage Plan with all the actuals
- Project Plan outlook
- Business Case review
- Risk review
- Project Issue situation
- Quality checking statistics
- Report on any internal or external events that have affected stage performance.

Form(at)

Site report standards covering the information described above plus any extra requested by the Project Board.

Derivation

Information for the report is obtained from:

- The Stage Plan and actuals
- The next Stage Plan (if appropriate)
- The updated Project Plan
- The Lessons Learned Log
- Data from the Quality Log
- Completed Work Package data.

Quality Criteria

- Does it clearly describe stage performance against the plan?
- Were any approved modifications described, together with their impact?
- Does it give an accurate picture of the quality testing work done in the stage?
- Does it give an accurate review of the revised risk situation?
- Does it give an accurate assessment of the ability of the project to meet its Business Case?

Quality Method

Informal Quality Review between Project Manager and those with Project Assurance responsibility.

Title

Exception Report

Purpose

An Exception Report is produced when costs and/or timescales for an approved Stage Plan are forecast to exceed the tolerance levels set. It is sent by the Project Manager in order to warn the Project Board of the adverse situation.

An Exception Report may result in the Project Board asking the Project Manager to produce an Exception Plan.

Composition

- A description of the cause of the deviation from the Stage Plan

- The consequences of the deviation

- The available options

- The effect of each option on the Business Case, risks, project and stage tolerances

- The Project Manager's recommendations.

Form(at)

Site report standard containing the information shown above.

Derivation

The information for an Exception Report is drawn from:

- Current Stage Plan and actuals

- Project Plan and actuals

- Deviation forecast

- Issue Log
- Risk Log
- Quality Log
- Checkpoint Reports
- Project Board advice of an external event that affects the project.

Quality Criteria

- The Exception Report must accurately show the current status of stage and project budget and schedule, plus the forecast impact on both of the deviations
- The reason(s) for the deviation must be stated
- Options, including 'do nothing', must be put forward, together with their impact on objectives, plans, Business Case and risks
- A recommendation must be made.

Quality Method

Informal review between Project Manager, any Team Managers and those with Project Assurance responsibility.

Title

Follow-on Action Recommendations

Purpose

To pass details of any unfinished work, outstanding risks or unresolved Project Issues to the group charged with support of the final product in its operational life.

Composition

- Date of the recommendations
- Project Issues which were unresolved at the time of project closure
- Risks identified during the project that may affect the product in its operational life
- Ongoing training needs
- Any other activities identified for possible action in the operational life of the product.

Form(at)

Site report standard containing the information shown above.

Derivation

- Issue Log
- Risk Log.

Quality Criteria

- There must be an entry for every open Project Issue

- The relevant Project Issues should have been closed with an entry pointing to the Follow-on Action Recommendations

- Any available useful documentation should accompany the recommendation.

Quality Method

Informal review between Project Manager and those with Project Assurance responsibility.

Title
Highlight Report

Purpose

For the Project Manager to provide the Project Board with a summary of the stage status at intervals defined by them in the Project Initiation Document.

A Highlight Report normally summarises a series of Checkpoint Reports. The Project Board uses the report to monitor stage and project progress. The Project Manager also uses it to advise the Project Board of any potential problems or areas where the Project Board could help.

Composition

- Date
- Project
- Stage
- Period covered
- Budget status
- Schedule status
- Products completed during the period
- Actual or potential problems
- Products to be completed during the next period
- Project Issue status
- Budget and schedule impact of any changes approved so far in the stage.

Form(at)

Site reporting standards containing the above information plus any extra data requested by the Project Board.

Derivation

Information for the Highlight Reports is derived from:

- Checkpoint Reports
- Stage Plan
- The Issue Log
- The Risk Log.

Quality Criteria

- Accurate reflection of Checkpoint Reports
- Accurate summary of the Issue Log status
- Accurate summary of the Stage Plan status
- Highlights any potential problem areas.

Quality Method

Informal review between the Project Manager and those with Project Assurance responsibility.

Title

Issue Log

Purpose

The purpose of the Issue Log is to:

- Allocate a unique number to each Project Issue
- Record the type of Project Issue
- Be a summary of the Project Issues, their analysis and status.

Composition

- Project Issue number
- Project Issue type (Issue, Request for Change, Off-Specification)
- Summary of the issue
- Author
- Date created
- Date of last update
- Status
- Cross-reference to the filed Project Issue.

Form(at)

Standard department form with the headings shown under 'Composition'.

Derivation

Project Issues may be raised by anyone associated with the project at any time.

Quality Criteria

- Does the status indicate whether action has been taken?
- Are the Project Issues uniquely identified, including to which product they refer?
- Is access to the Issue Log controlled?
- Is the Issue Log kept in a safe place?

Quality Method

Regular inspection and verification against the filed Project Issues.

Title

Lessons Learned Log

Purpose

The purpose of the Lessons Learned Log is to be a repository of any lessons learned during the project that can be usefully applied to other projects. At the close of the project it is written up formally in the Lessons Learned Report. Minimally it should be updated at the end of a stage, but sensibly a note should be made in it of any good or bad point that arises in the use of the management and specialist products and tools at the time of the experience.

Composition

What management and quality processes:

- Went well
- Went badly
- Were lacking.

A description of any abnormal events causing deviations.

Notes on the performance of specialist methods and tools used.

Recommendations for future enhancement or modification of the project management method.

Useful measurements on how much effort was required to create the various products.

Notes on effective and ineffective Quality Reviews and other tests, including the reasons for them working well or badly.

Derivation

Information for the report is derived from:

- Observation and experience of the processes

- The Quality Log
- Completed Work Packages
- Stage Plans with actuals.

Quality Criteria

- Each management control has been considered
- The reasons for all tolerance deviations and corrective actions have been recorded
- Input to the log is being done, minimally, at the end of each stage
- Project Assurance and Project Support have been asked for their input
- Every specialist technique is included
- Statistics of the success of Quality Reviews and other types of test used are included.

Title

Lessons Learned Report

Purpose

The purpose of the Lessons Learned Report is to pass on to other projects any useful lessons that can be learned from this project.

An independent group, such as quality assurance, who are responsible for the site quality management system, to refine, change and improve project management and technical standards, should use the data in the report. Statistics on how much effort was needed for products can help improve future estimating.

Composition

- What management and quality processes:
  - Went well
  - Went badly
  - Were lacking.
- An assessment of the efficacy of technical methods and tools used
- Recommendations for future enhancement or modification of the project management method, including the reasons
- Measurements on how much effort was required to create the various products
- A description of any abnormal events causing deviations to targets or plans
- An analysis of Project Issues raised, their causes and results
- Statistics on how effective Quality Reviews and other tests were in error trapping (e.g. how many errors were found after products had passed a Quality Review or test).

Form(at)

Site reporting standards containing at least the above information.

Derivation

Information for the report is derived from:

- Observation and experience of the processes and techniques used
- Checkpoint Reports
- Observations of quality checks
- Performance against plans
- End Stage Reports
- Any exception situations.

Quality Criteria

- Input to the report is being done, minimally, at the end of each stage
- Every management control has been examined
- A review of every specialist technique is included
- Statistics of the success of Quality Reviews and other types of quality check used are included
- The accuracy of all estimates and plans is included
- Details of the effort taken for each product are given
- The success of change control is reviewed.

Quality Method

Informal review at each stage end by the Project Manager and those with Project Assurance responsibility.

Formal Quality Review by this group before presentation.

Title

Off-Specification

Purpose

An Off-Specification is a specific type of Project Issue. It is used to document any situation where a product or the project is failing, or is forecast to fail, to meet a target.

Composition

Same composition as a Project Issue.

Form(at)

Same format as Project Issue.

Derivation

Can be raised by anyone associated with the project at any time.

Quality Criteria

- Logged in the Issue Log
- Accurate description of the problem.

Quality Method

Form completion checked by the person responsible for the Issue Log.

Checked on a regular basis by the persons responsible for customer and supplier Project Assurance.

Title

Post-Project Review

Purpose

The purpose of the Post-Project Review is to find out:

- Whether the expected benefits of the product have been realised
- If the product has caused any problems in use
- What enhancement opportunities have been revealed by use of the product.

Each expected benefit is assessed for the level of its achievement so far and any additional time needed for the benefit to materialise.

Unexpected side effects, beneficial or adverse, which use of the product may have brought, are documented with explanations of why these were not foreseen.

Recommendations are made to realise or improve benefits, or counter problems.

Composition

- Achievement of expected benefits
- Unexpected benefits
- Unexpected problems
- User reaction
- Follow-on work recommendations.

Form(at)

Site reporting standards.

Derivation

The expected benefits should have been defined in the Project Brief and expanded in the Project Initiation Document.

General comments should be obtained about how the users feel about the product. The type of observation will depend on the type of product produced by the project, but examples might be its ease of use, performance, reliability, contribution it makes to their work, and suitability for the work environment.

Quality Criteria

- Covers all benefits mentioned in the Project Brief and Business Case

- Covers all changes approved during the project life cycle

- Includes discussions with representatives of all those affected by the end product

- Describes each achievement in a tangible, measurable form

- Makes recommendations in cases where a benefit is not being fully provided, a problem has been identified, or a potential extra benefit could be obtained

- Is conducted as soon as the benefits and problems can be measured.

Quality Method

Formal Quality Review against the Project Brief, Business Case and Issue Log.

Title

Post-Project Review Plan

Purpose

The purpose of the Post-Project Review Plan is to define for the Executive how and when a measurement of the achievement of the project benefits can be made. The plan is presented to the Executive at the end of the project.

The plan has to cover the effort to find out:

- Whether the expected benefits of the product have been realised
- Whether the product has caused any problems in use.

Each expected benefit has to be assessed for the level of its achievement so far, or any additional time needed for the benefit to materialise. Use of the product may have brought unexpected side effects, either beneficial or adverse. Time and effort have to be allowed to document explanations of why these side effects were not foreseen. The plan must include time for recommendations on how to realise or improve benefits, or counter problems.

Composition

- How to measure achievement of expected benefits
- When the various benefits can be measured
- What resources are needed to carry out the review work
- A pointer to other headings that will need to be covered, such as user reaction.

Derivation

- The Business Case
- Discussion with the users and product support people

- The Post-Project Review is planned as part of 'Identifying Follow-on Actions'(CP2), but the Executive produces the review itself after the project has finished.

Quality Criteria

- Covers all benefits mentioned in the Business Case

- Describes a suitable timing for measurement of the benefits, together with reasons

- Identifies the skills or individuals who will be needed to carry out the measurements

- Is realistic in terms of effort when compared to the anticipated benefits.

Title

Product Breakdown Structure

Purpose

To show all products to be developed and quality controlled. To understand the content and function of all products to be developed.

Composition

Top-to-bottom diagram showing breakdown of all products to be developed. External products must be clearly distinguished from the products developed by the project. The usual PRINCE2 convention is for project products to be shown as rectangles and external products as ellipses.

Some products are resulting from the integration of other products (such as a car chassis subassembly). If the integration requires extra development or quality control activity then the 'super-product' must be distinguished in some way (e.g. a line across the top-left corner of the product box).

Derivation

- Project Brief
- Project Quality Plan.

Quality Criteria

- Are all external products and project products clearly identified and distinguished?
- Is the PBS consistent with the Product Checklist?
- Are genuine super-products (i.e. non-bottom level but requiring a separate product description) distinguished from convenient product groupings (memory joggers)?

- Are management and specialist products identified and distinguished?

- Can product descriptions for the bottom level products be written without further decomposition?

- Have enough bottom-level products been identified to meet management control requirements?

- Will all the products identified fulfil the business need?

- Have all quality products that meet the needs of customer, audit and quality assurance as described in the Project Quality Plan been identified?

- Is the numbering of each product unique and consistent with the level of the product in the hierarchy?

- Has responsibility for the monitoring of the quality of external products been clearly identified?

Title

Product Checklist

Purpose

Lists the products to be produced within a plan, together with key status dates.

Updated at agreed reporting intervals by the Project Manager and used by the Project Board to monitor progress.

Composition

- Plan identification
- Product names (and identifiers where appropriate)
- Planned and actual dates for:
  - Draft product ready
  - Quality check
  - Approval.

Form(at)

Standard department form with the headings defined under 'Composition'.

Derivation

Extracted from the Stage Plan.

Quality Criteria

Do the details and dates match those in the Stage Plan?

Quality Method

Informal review against the Stage Plan.

Title

Product Description

Purpose

To define the information needed to describe each product to be created by the project.

Composition

- Title

- Purpose.
  An explanation of the purpose of the product.

- Composition.
  A list of the various parts of the product, e.g. chapters of the document.

- Form or format.
  What the product should look like. If it is a document, the name of the template to be used.

- Derivation.
  The sources of information for the product.

- Quality Criteria.
  What quality measurements the product must meet.

- Quality Method.
  What method of checking the product's quality is to be used, and what type of skill is required.

Form(at)

Standard department form with the headings defined under 'Composition'.

Derivation

- Project Brief
- Project Initiation Document
- Project Quality Plan
- Ultimate recipient of the product.

Quality Criteria

- Does it contain information under all the headings?
- Is there more than one purpose?
- Has the end user been involved in its writing?

Quality Method

Formal Quality Review.

Title

Product Flow Diagram

Purpose

To show the required sequence of delivery of a plan's products and identify dependencies between those products, including any external products.

Composition

A diagram showing the product delivery sequence from top to bottom or left to right, plus the dependencies between those products. Arrows indicate dependencies between products. External products must be clearly distinguished from the products developed by the plan. The normal PRINCE2 convention is for project products to be shown as rectangles and external products as ellipses.

Derivation

Product Descriptions (derivation field) and Product Breakdown Structure (external products).

Quality Criteria

- Are all external products identified and the dependencies understood?

- Are all bottom-level products on the PBS identified on the diagram?

- Are all 'super-products' identified on the PBS shown on the PFD?

- Are all products identified in the PFD identified as products on the PBS?

- Are there any products without dependencies?

- Have dependencies been identified at a level suitable to that of the plan of which the PFD is a part?

- Are the dependencies consistent with the derivation fields (from Product Description) of all the products?

Title

Project Approach

Purpose

Defines the type of solution to be developed or procured by the project. It should also identify the environment into which the product must be delivered.

Composition

- Type of solution, e.g.:
  - Off-the-shelf
  - Built from scratch
  - Modifying an existing product
  - Built by one or more external suppliers
  - Adding to/modifying a product developed by another project
  - Built by company staff
  - Built by contract staff under the supervision of the Project Manager.
- Reason for the selection of approach, e.g. part of a programme
- Implications on the project.

Form(at)

Standard department form with the headings defined under 'Composition'.

Derivation

- Project Brief
- Design Authority (if part of a programme)
- Available solutions on offer.

Quality Criteria

- Must support the business strategy
- Must relate to the product's operational environment
- Must be achievable within the known project constraints
- The approach implications must be acceptable to the programme (if the project is part of one).

Quality Method

Formal Quality Review against the business strategy, any other relevant user strategies and the operational environment.

Title

Project Brief

Purpose

To briefly explain the reasons for the project, the customer's expectations, and any limitations which apply.

Composition

The following is a suggested list of contents that should be tailored to the requirements and environment of each project:

- Project Definition, explaining what the project needs to achieve:
  - Background
  - Project objectives
  - Project scope
  - Outline project deliverables and/or desired outcomes
  - Any exclusions
  - Constraints
  - Interfaces.
- Outline Business Case
  - reason for the project
  - description of how this project supports business strategy, plans or programmes
- Customer's Quality Expectations
- Acceptance Criteria
- Any known risks.

If earlier work has been done, the Project Brief may refer to document(s), such as Outline Project Plan.

Form(at)

Site project request standards containing at least the information shown above.

Derivation

- Project Mandate
- If the project is part of a programme, the programme should provide the Project Brief
- If no Project Mandate is provided, the Project Manager has to generate the Project Brief in discussions with the customer and users
- Any significant change to the material contained in the Project Brief will thus need to be referred to corporate or programme management.

Quality Criteria

- Does it accurately reflect the Project Mandate?
- Does it form a firm basis on which to initiate a project (Initiating a Project (IP))?
- Does it indicate how the customer will assess the acceptability of the finished product(s)?

Quality Method

Informal Quality Review between Project Manager and Project Board during the process 'Starting Up a Project' (SU).

Title

Project Initiation Document

Purpose

- To define the project
- To form the basis for the ultimate assessment of the project's success and the project's management.

There are two primary uses of the document:

- To ensure that the project has a sound basis before asking the Project Board to make any major commitment to the project
- To act as a base document against which the Project Board and Project Manager can assess progress, evaluate change issues and question the project's continuing viability.

Composition

The Project Initiation Document must answer the following fundamental questions:

- **What** the project is aiming to achieve
- **Why** it is important to achieve it
- **Who** is going to be involved in managing the project and what is their responsibility
- **How** and **when** it is all going to happen.

The following list should be seen as the information needed in order to make the initiation decisions.

- **Background,** explaining the context of the project, and steps taken to arrive at the current position of requiring a project
- **Project Definition,** explaining what the project needs to achieve. Under this heading may be:

- Project objectives

- Project deliverables and/or desired outcomes

- Project scope

- Constraints

- Exclusions

- Defined method of approach (if applicable)

- Interfaces.

- **Assumptions**

- **Initial Business Case,** explaining why the project is being undertaken

- **Project Organisation Structure,** defining the Project Management Team

- **Project Quality Plan** (See the separate Project Quality Plan Product Description.)

- **Initial Project Plan**, explaining how and when the activities of the project will occur. (For details of the Project Plan content see the separate Product Description.)

- **Project Controls,** stating how control is to be exercised within the project, and the reporting and monitoring mechanisms that will support this

- **Exception process,** the steps to be followed for any significant deviations

- **Initial Risk Log,** summarising the results of the risk analysis and risk management activities

- **Contingency Plans,** explaining how it is intended to deal with the consequences of any identified serious risks if they materialise

- **Project Filing Structure,** laying down how the various elements of information and deliverables produced by the project are to be filed and retrieved.

Form(at)
Site report standards.

Derivation

- Customer's or supplier's project management standards
- Customer's specified control requirements.

(Much of the information should come from the Project Mandate, enhanced in the Project Brief.)

Quality Criteria

- Does the document correctly represent the project?

- Does it show a viable, achievable project that is in line with corporate strategy, or overall programme needs?

- Is the project organisation structure complete, with names and titles?

- Does it clearly show a control, reporting and direction regime that can be implemented and is appropriate to the scale, business risk and importance of the project?

- Has everyone named in the organisation structure received and accepted their job description?

- Does the project organisation structure need to say to whom the Project Board reports?

- Are the internal and external relationships and lines of authority clear?

- Do the controls cover the needs of the Project Board, Project Manager and any Team Managers?

- Do the controls satisfy any delegated Project Assurance requirements?

- Is it clear who will administer each control?

Quality Method

Formal Quality Review between the Project Manager and those with Project Assurance responsibility.

Title

Project Issue

Purpose

To record any matter which has to be brought to the attention of the project, and requires an answer. A Project Issue may be a:

- Request for Change
- Off-Specification
- Question
- Statement of concern.

Composition

- Author
- Date
- Issue number
- Description of the issue
- Priority
- Impact analysis
- Decision
- Signature of decision maker(s)
- Date of decision.

Form(at)

Department style of form with the headings shown under 'Composition'.

Derivation

Anyone may submit a Project Issue. Typical sources are users and specialists working on the project, the Project Manager and those with Project Assurance responsibility.

Quality Criteria

- Is the statement of the problem/requirement clear?
- Has all necessary information been made available?
- Have all the implications been considered?
- Has the Project Issue been correctly logged?

Quality Method

Check by the person responsible for the Issue Log.

Title

Project Mandate

Purpose

Project Mandate is a term to describe an initial request for a project, which may require further work to turn it into a Project Brief.

Composition

The actual composition of a Project Mandate will vary according to the type and size of project and also the environment in which the mandate is generated.

The following is a list of contents that would make up an 'ideal' mandate, and should be tailored to suit the specific project. An actual mandate may have much less information.

- Authority responsible
- The customer(s), user(s) and any other known interested parties
- Background
- Outline Business Case (reasons)
- Project objectives
- Scope
- Constraints
- Interfaces
- Quality expectations
- An estimate of the project size and duration (if known)
- A view of the risks faced by the project
- An indication of who should be the project Executive and Project Manager
- Reference to any associated projects or products.

Form(at)

May be in any form.

Derivation

A Project Mandate may come from anywhere, but it should come from a level of management that can authorise the cost and resource usage.

Quality Criteria

- Does the mandate describe what is required?
- Is the level of authority commensurate with the anticipated size, risk and cost of the project?
- Is there sufficient detail to allow the appointment of an appropriate Executive and Project Manager?
- Are all the known interested parties identified?

Quality Method

Informal review between Executive, Project Manager and the mandate author.

Title

Project Plan

Purpose

A mandatory plan which shows at a high level how and when a project's objectives are to be achieved. It contains the major products of the project, the activities and resources required.

It provides the Business Case with planned project costs, and identifies the management stages and other major control points.

The Project Board uses it as a baseline against which to monitor project progress and cost stage by stage.

It forms part of the Project Initiation Document.

Composition

- Plan description, giving a brief description of what the plan covers
- Project prerequisites, containing any fundamental aspects that must be in place at the start of the project, and that must remain in place for the project to succeed
- External dependencies
- Planning assumptions
- Project Plan, covering:
  - Project level Gantt or bar chart with identified management stages
  - Project level Product Breakdown Structure
  - Project level Product Flow Diagrams
  - Project level Product Descriptions
  - Project level activity network

– Project financial budget

– Project level table of resource requirements

– Requested/assigned specific resources.

Form(at)

Gantt or bar chart plus text.

Derivation

Project Brief.

Quality Criteria

- Is the plan achievable?

- Does it support the rest of the Project Initiation Document?

Quality Method

Formal Quality Review with Project Manager and those with Project Assurance responsibility.

Title

Project Quality Plan

Purpose

The purpose is to define how the supplier intends to deliver products that meet the Customer's Quality Expectations and the agreed quality standards.

Composition

- Quality control and audit processes to be applied to project management

- Quality control and audit process requirements for specialist work

- Key product quality criteria

- Quality responsibilities

- Reference to any standards that need to be met

- Change management procedures

- Configuration management plan

- Any tools to be used to ensure quality.

Form(at)

The Project Quality Plan is part of the Project Initiation Document.

Derivation

- Customer's Quality Expectations (Project Mandate and/or Brief)

- Corporate or programme quality management system (QMS).

Quality Criteria

- Does the plan clearly define ways to confirm that the Customer's Quality Expectations will be met?

- Are the defined ways sufficient to achieve the required quality?

- Are responsibilities for quality defined up to a level that is independent of the project and Project Manager?

- Does the plan conform to corporate quality policy?

Quality Method

Review between Project Manager and whoever is assuring the project on behalf of the customer.

Title

Quality Log

Purpose

- To issue a unique reference for each quality check or test planned

- To act as a pointer to the quality check and test documentation for a product

- To act as a summary of the number and type of quality checks and tests held.

The log summarises all the quality checks and tests that are planned/ have taken place, and provides information for the End Stage and End Project Reports, as well as the Lessons Learned Report.

Composition

For each entry in the log:

- Quality check reference number

- Product checked or tested

- Planned date of the check

- Actual date of the check

- Result of the check

- Number of action items found

- Target sign-off date

- Actual sign-off date.

Form(at)

Standard departmental form with the headings shown in 'Composition'.

Derivation

The first entries are made when a quality check or test is entered on a Stage Plan. The remaining information comes from the actual performance of the check. The sign-off date is when all corrective action items have been signed off.

Quality Criteria

- Is there a procedure in place which will ensure that every quality check is entered on the log?

- Has responsibility for the log been allocated?

Quality Method

Regular checking should be done by those with Project Assurance responsibility for the customer and provider. There may also be an inspection by an independent quality assurance function.

Title

Request for Change

Purpose

To request a modification to a product or an acceptance criterion as currently specified.

Composition

- Date
- Issue Log number
- Class
- Status
- Description of the proposed change
- Impact of the change
- Priority assessment
- Decision
- Allocation details, if applicable
- Date allocated
- Date completed.

Form(at)

The same form as the Project Issue.

Derivation

Anyone connected with the project.

Quality Criteria

- Source of the request clearly identified
- Logged in the Issue Log
- Accurate description of the requested change
- Supported by any necessary evidence
- Benefit of making the change clearly expressed and, where possible, in measurable terms.

Quality Method

Initial review by those with Project Assurance responsibility, if any of these are delegated by the Project Board. Confirmation of the type by the Project Manager.

Title
Risk Log

Purpose
The purpose of the Risk Log is to:

- Allocate a unique number to each risk
- Record the type of risk
- Be a summary of the risks, their analysis and status.

Composition

- Risk number
- Risk type (business, project, stage)
- Author
- Date risk identified
- Date of last risk status update
- Risk description
- Likelihood
- Severity
- Countermeasure(s)
- Status
- Responsibility.

Form(at)
Standard department form with the headings shown in 'Composition'.

Derivation

Business risks may have been identified in the Project Brief and should be sought during project initiation. There should be a check for any new risks every time the Risk Log is reviewed or a new plan made, minimally at each end stage assessment. The Project Board has the responsibility to constantly check external events for risks.

Quality Criteria

- Does the status indicate whether action has been/is being taken or is in a contingency plan?

- Are the risks uniquely identified, including to which product they refer?

- Is access to the Risk Log controlled?

- Is the Risk Log kept in a safe place?

- Are activities to review the Risk Log in the Stage Plans?

- Has responsibility for monitoring the risk been identified and documented?

Quality Method

Regular review by the person who has business assurance responsibility.

Title

Stage Plan

Purpose

- Identifies the products that the stage must produce
- Provides a statement of how and when a stage's objectives are to be achieved
- Identifies the stage's control and reporting points and frequencies
- Provides a baseline against which stage progress will be measured
- Records the stage tolerances
- Specifies the quality controls for the stage and the resources needed for them.

Composition

- Plan Description
- Stage Quality Plan
- Plan Prerequisites
- External Dependencies
- Tolerances (time and budget)
- How will the plan be monitored and controlled?
- Reporting
- Planning Assumptions
- Graphical Plan, showing identified resources, activities, start and end dates (usually a Gantt or bar chart)
- Financial budget

- Table of resource requirements
- Risk assessment
- Product Descriptions for the major products.

Form(at)

Graphical plan plus text.

Derivation

- Project Plan
- Based on resource availability.

Quality Criteria

- Is the plan achievable?
- Do any Team Managers involved in its operation believe that their portion is achievable?
- Does it support the Project Plan?
- Does it take into account any constraints of time, resources and budget?
- Has it been taken down to the level of detail necessary to ensure that any deviations will be recognised in time to react appropriately? (For example, within the stage tolerances, and within the activity 'floats'.)
- Has it been developed according to the planning standard?
- Does the Stage Plan contain activities and resource effort to review the Issue Log?

Quality Method

Review by the Project Manager and those with Project Assurance responsibility.

Title

Work Package

Purpose

A set of instructions to produce one or more required products given by the Project Manager to a Team Manager or team member.

Composition

Although the content may vary greatly according to the relationship between the Project Manager and the recipient of the Work Package, it should cover:

- A summary of the work to be done
- Product Description(s) of the products to be produced
- Standards to be used
- Product interfaces
- Working interfaces and liaisons
- Quality checking standards, personnel to be involved
- Reporting requirements
- Work return arrangements.

Form(at)

This product will vary in content and in degree of formality, depending on circumstances. Where the work is being conducted by a single team working directly for the Project Manager, the Work Package may be a verbal instruction, although there are good reasons for putting it in writing, such as avoidance of misunderstanding and providing a link to performance assessment. Where a supplier under a contract is carrying out the work and the Project

Manager is part of the customer organisation, the Work Package should be a formal, written document.

Derivation

There could be many Work Packages authorised during each stage. The Project Manager creates a Work Package from the Stage Plan.

Quality Criteria

- Is the required Work Package clearly defined and understood by the assigned resource?
- Is there a Product Description for the required product(s) with clearly identified and acceptable quality criteria?
- Does the Product Description match up with the other Work Package documentation?
- Are standards for the work agreed?
- Are the defined standards in line with those applied to similar products?
- Have all necessary interfaces been defined?
- Do the reporting arrangements include the provision for exception reporting?

Quality Method

Agreement between Project Manager and recipient.

Appendix 2   Forms

This appendix contains samples of many of the forms you will need in a PRINCE2 project. They are there to give you an idea of what to put in your forms and how the forms might be structured. Feel free to either use them as they are or modify them to suit your environment.

Any text in *italics* is there to guide you on what to put under a heading. Any text in **bold** could form a suggested entry in your document.

Business Case

PURPOSE OF DOCUMENT

This document is used to justify the undertaking of the *xyz* project and is based on the estimated cost of development and the anticipated business benefits to be gained.

It states why the forecast effort and time will be worth the expenditure. The ongoing viability of this project is to be monitored by the Project Board against this Business Case.

Note that this document is at a fairly high level when first produced. It should be enhanced during the Project Start-Up stage and finalised during the process 'Initiating a Project'. From then on it should be maintained to reflect any changes outside of agreed tolerances.

REASONS

The reasons for the project should be stated here and derived from information contained in the Project Mandate/Project Brief.

BENEFITS

This section should indicate what the benefits are and how they are justified. Much of this information will be derived from the Project Mandate/Project Brief and the Customer.

COST AND TIMESCALES

This section should be presented in the format of a spreadsheet if necessary.

INVESTMENT APPRAISAL

Checkpoint Report

FOLLOW-UPS
The follow-up actions from previous reports.

PRODUCTS COMPLETED
A description of the products completed since the last checkpoint.

QUALITY
The quality checks performed this period.

RISK STATUS
New or modified risks.

PROBLEMS
Actual or potential problems/deviations from plans encountered in this period.

PRODUCTS TO BE COMPLETED IN THE NEXT PERIOD
The products planned to be completed during the next period.

End Project Report

PURPOSE OF DOCUMENT

The purpose of this document is to enable the Project Manager to report to the Project Board on how well the project has performed against its Project Initiation Document, including the original planned costs, schedule and tolerances, the revised Business Case and the final version of the Project Plan.

The following sections should be derived from information contained in:

- Updated Project Plan
- Project Initiation Document
- Business Case
- Issues Log.

ACHIEVEMENT

A statement of the project's objectives and their respective levels of achievement.

PERFORMANCE

Performance against the planned target time and cost, including tolerance levels.

PROJECT CHANGES

Statistics

NUMBER OF APPROVED CHANGES	TIME	COST
Final statistics on change issues received during the project.	The effect on the original Project Plan timeframe of any changes that were approved during the project.	The effect on the original Project Cost of any changes that were approved during the project.

BUSINESS CASE IMPACT

The total impact of approved changes against the Savings and Benefits identified in the Project Initiation Document.

QUALITY

Statistics for all quality work carried out and confirmation that quality expectations of the customer have been met.

BENEFITS

State how progress against the realisation of benefits is being made. If benefits have not been achieved at this time, a Post-Project Review should be planned (see below).

POST-PROJECT REVIEW

The date and plan for any proposed review.

End Stage Report

SUMMARY

This document is a report of the *Stage Name* stage of the *Project Name* project. It describes what has happened in the stage and the overall effect it has had on the project.

The End Stage Report should be as succinct and brief as possible. Its purpose is to give the Project Board a clear picture of what has happened in the stage and define current project status. The next Stage Plan will contain the detail of what is to happen next.

MANAGEMENT SUMMARY

The purpose of this section is to summarise the contents of the report. It should mention key events, project impact, unresolved problems and any recommendations. Keep it brief.

STAGE DETAILS

The purpose of this section is to provide a comparison of the actual results of the stage with the planned results of the stage. The section is broken down into three parts.

Schedule/Resources

A tabular representation can be used as shown here:

	Plan	Actual	Difference	% Difference	Tolerance
Stage End Date				N/A	
Stage Effort (m/days)					
Stage Cost (£)					

Product Status

All that is required is a confirmation of the products that have been delivered, e.g. 'All required products were delivered within the Stage budget and schedule tolerances.' Any products not delivered should be identified.

Problems

If products have not been delivered or there are problems then more detail should be supplied here.

PROJECT ISSUE STATUS

The overall number of Project Issues dealt with during the stage can be presented as a table similar to the one shown here:

	Brought Forward	Received	Actioned	Rejected	Carried Forward
Issues					
RFC					
OS					

(RFC = Request for Change; OS = Off-Specification)

Project Issues requiring Project Board decisions should be listed and BRIEFLY described.

PROJECT MANAGEMENT REASSESSMENT

The purpose of this section is to illustrate the impact of completed stages on the Project Plan, Business Case and Risks. The section is broken down into three parts.

Project Plan Impact

A tabular representation can be used as shown here:

	Original	Forecast	Difference	% Difference	Tolerance
Project End Date				N/A	
Project Effort (m/days)					
Project Cost (£)					

Business Case Impact

Identify any changes to the expected benefits caused by the completed stage or confirm that the Business Case expectations have not changed.

Risk Impact

Identify any changes to expected risks arising during the completed stage and any new risks that have arisen. Refer to the elements of the next Stage Plan, which are there to counter or take advantage of any change.

INTERIM PROJECT EVALUATION

*The purpose of this section is to document any lessons learned during the stage. An End Project Report is presented to the **Steering Committee** at project closure. This section will contribute to the **Steering Committee's** understanding of the next Stage Plan and provide reference information for the Project Manager when compiling the report.*

Exception Report

PURPOSE OF DOCUMENT

The purpose of this report is to highlight to the Project Board that one or more tolerances for an approved Stage or Project Plan are forecast to be exceeded.

DEVIATION

Identify the plan from which the deviation is forecast. Describe the cause of the deviation including current status of budget, schedule, scope and quality.

CONSEQUENCES

Describe the consequences of the deviation.

OPTIONS

Describe the options available to resolve the problem and the effect of each option on the Business Case, risks, project and stage tolerances.

RECOMMENDATION

The Project Manager's recommendation on the best option to proceed with.

Highlight Report

FOLLOW-UPS

The follow-up actions from previous reports.

PRODUCTS COMPLETED

A description of the products completed since the last checkpoint.

QUALITY

The quality checks performed this period.

RISK STATUS

New or modified risks.

PROBLEMS

Actual or potential problems/deviations from plans encountered in this period.

PRODUCTS TO BE COMPLETED IN THE NEXT PERIOD

The products planned to be completed during the next period.

Project Issues Actioned		Cost of Actioned Project Issues	
Project Issues Still Open		Schedule Impact of Actioned Project Issues	

Project Brief

INTRODUCTION

The purpose of this section is to describe the Project Brief itself. It will include a statement of the general reasons for producing a Brief, as well as a project specific description of its purpose.

The reasons for the level of detail in the document should be given. The level may depend on how much information is available at the time of producing the Brief, or it may depend on the level requested. A very small or low risk project will require less detail than a major or strategic project.

SUMMARY

This document describes the background, objectives, scope and outline Business Case of the *Project Name* project.

BACKGROUND

The purpose of this section is to put the project in context by describing where it fits in the scheme of things. It will contain a brief high level description of the background to the project and relevant historical and strategic information.

There should be a brief statement of the problem/opportunity/requirement that the project is to address, and an indication of how it fits with the business strategy.

References should be made to existing documentation rather than reproducing it.

PROJECT OBJECTIVES

*The purpose of this paragraph is to state the objectives of the **project**, which should not be confused with the objectives of the products it is to deliver.*

For example, the objectives of the New PC Project are:

- *To make available a standard, cost-effective PC configuration to customers by 31 January 1999*

- *To put in place a procurement method that takes advantage of the standardisation to reduce prices and delivery times.*

In order to do this, the project will deliver the products described below.

SCOPE

Deliverables

Identify the systems and major products that will be created, modified or removed by the project.

Exclusions

In essence, the deliverables in the previous paragraph define the boundaries of the project. It may be necessary to state the things that the project will not create, modify or remove, if a reasonable assumption could be made that the project will, in fact, include them.

OUTLINE BUSINESS CASE

The purpose of this section is to document the justification for the project. It will be based upon the underlying business problem or opportunity that the project is to address.

Any information known or mandated about the timescale, effort and cost objectives of the project should be stated.

For large, high risk projects, a cost/benefit analysis and investment appraisal showing costs, benefits and cash flow for the project will be required in the Terms of Reference. The basics of these figures may have been created in some earlier study. If so, they should be included here.

For smaller, low risk projects, a simple statement of why the project is required may suffice.

If there is a separate document containing the Business Case, say from a Feasibility Study, then a summary or a reference to it will be sufficient.

Benefits may accrue from simply delivering the products or, more likely, they will only materialise through operation of the products.

CONSTRAINTS

The purpose of this paragraph is to describe the constraints within which the project must operate. Constraints such as those listed below should be identified:

- *Limitations imposed by management*

- *Implementation or other fixed dates*

- *Recognition of financial year or tax year*

- *Hardware platform*

- *Software platform*

- *Ministerial decree*

- *Limit on resources*

- *Limit on costs.*

Any restrictions (either management or technical) on the project's freedom to manoeuvre must be recorded.

PROJECT INTERDEPENDENCIES

*The purpose of this paragraph is to describe the things upon which the project will depend **during its life cycle**. Dependencies of other projects upon this project as well as the dependencies of this project on other projects should be included.*

If the project is dependent on external products, then they must be identified and monitored. Since there is no direct control over these external products some means of monitoring their progress or availability must be established and described here. For each external product required by the project as much of the following information as is currently available should be identified:

- *The product name*

- *The project products dependent on it*

- *Who is responsible for supplying or producing it*

- *When it is expected*

- *When it is required.*

As well as products you should consider such things as:

- *Conformance to existing operational systems*

- *Conformance to existing functions and procedures*

- *Release of staff from another project*

- *Policy formulation from another area of the business*

- *Conformance to strategies and standards*

- *Customer and supplier management interfaces.*

PRODUCT INTERDEPENDENCIES

This is a description of the interdependencies that will exist between the project's products after they have been delivered and those of other projects, operational systems or line management functions.

Other projects may depend on the products of this project. These interdependencies should also be identified.

QUALITY EXPECTATIONS

The purpose of this section is to define overall quality expectations by describing criteria that will be used to judge the success of the project and its products. Criteria should be measurable against some kind of yardstick.

Examples of criteria include:

- *Delivered on time*

- *Delivered to cost*
- *Productivity*
- *Functional requirements met*
- *Accepted by customer*
- *Product performance*
- *Reliability*
- *Maintainability*
- *User friendliness*
- *Security and control.*

KEY BUSINESS RISKS

The purpose of this section is to list and describe any known key risks to the project's Business Case and to indicate, where possible, the countermeasures needed to eliminate or minimise their impact. For each risk there should be:

Risk – *A description of the risk.*
Probability – *The chance of its occurrence (high/medium/low)*
Impact – *A description of the consequences of the risk actually occurring.*
Counter – *Any thoughts on what could be done to reduce the chances of the risk occurring or to minimise its impact if it does occur.*

The overall risk to which the implemented product, or lack of it, exposes the company should also be made clear.

PROJECT PLAN

There may be an estimate of project duration and cost from a previous study. If so, it should be confirmed as achievable before inclusion in this Brief.

TOLERANCES

Corporate or programme management should indicate to the Project Board what tolerance is to be allowed to the total project in terms of budget and schedule. If there is no earlier estimate of duration and cost, senior management may not yet have set the tolerances. This should be stated and tolerances established as part of the Project Initiation Document.

Project Issue

Issue Log No:	Date Raised:	
Author:	Status:	
Description:		
Technical Impact:		
Business Impact:		
Priority Assessment:		
Decision:	Authority:	Date:
Allocation Details (if applicable):		
Date Allocated:	Date Completed:	

Stage Plan

PURPOSE OF DOCUMENT

This document provides a statement of how and when the project stage objectives are to be achieved, by showing the major products, activities and resources required for the stage.

Define the purpose of the plan and describe its basis and format. Every attempt should be made to keep the plan as brief as possible.

PLAN DESCRIPTION

A brief description of what the stage covers. Put the Stage Plan into an overall project context and describe its relationship with the previous and subsequent stages. There should also be a list of the major specialist products to be produced in the stage, a statement of the stage start and end dates and the expected resource usage (by resource type).

Products carried over from the previous stage(s) should be identified together with their impact (schedule and resource) on the current stage and the overall project.

Any unusual events or situations that have influenced the contents of the plan should be described here.

TOLERANCE

State the Project Board's tolerance requirements for the stage. Tolerance is normally associated with cost and time but the Project Board may require tolerance for scope, quality or possibly key dates.

CONTROLS

Define the level and frequency of the management controls that are to be applied during the stage. If there is no change from the Project Plan then a statement confirming this is sufficient. Controls should enable the appropriate level of management to:

- *Ensure that the stage is on schedule*

- *Ensure that the stage is within budget*

- *Ensure that products are delivered as planned*

- *Ensure that problems are anticipated and managed*

- *Ensure that change is controlled and that current product status is known*

- *Ensure that risks are managed*

- *Decide upon any necessary corrective action.*

STAGE PLANNING ASSUMPTIONS

State the key assumptions made during the stage planning process. If there is no change from the Project Plan then a statement confirming this will be sufficient. Mention the things that the plan will depend upon **during the stage** or assumes are in place when the stage begins.

PROJECT FORECAST

A description of the expected impact of the Stage Plan on the overall project.

PROJECT PLAN IMPACT

A tabular representation can be used as shown here. There is quite a lot of detail in this table. Try to include as much of it as possible.

	Plan-ned	**Actual**	Fore-cast	**Diff-erence**	% Difference	Tole-rance
Stage End Date	A	n/a	B	C	n/a	
Stage Effort (m/days)	D	n/a	E	F	G	
Stage Cost (£)	H	n/a	I	J	K	
Project End Date	L	n/a	M	N	n/a	
Project Effort (m/days)	O	P	Q	R	S	
Project Cost (£)	T	U	V	W	X	

Table entries are referenced below (A to X) and their contents explained. Where an entry is not applicable it is marked in the table 'n/a'.

- *A – the original stage End Date determined during project initiation and documented in the PID*

- *B – the stage End Date that is now forecast as the result of preparing this Stage Plan*

- *C – the difference between the Planned and Forecast stage End Dates in days, weeks or months*

- *D – the original effort for the stage determined during project initiation and documented in the PID*

- *E – the total stage Effort that is now forecast as the result of preparing this Stage Plan*

- *F – the difference between Planned and Forecast stage Effort (D–E)*

- *G – the difference between Planned and Forecast stage Effort (D–E) expressed as a percentage of the Planned stage Effort*

- *H – the original cost for the stage determined during project initiation and documented in the PID*

- *I – the total stage Cost that is now forecast as the result of preparing this Stage Plan*

- *J – the difference between Planned and Forecast stage Cost (H–I)*

- *K – the difference between Planned and Forecast stage Cost (H–I) expressed as a percentage of the Planned stage Cost*

- *L – the original Project End Date determined during project initiation and documented in the PID*

- *M – the Project End Date that is now forecast as the result of preparing this Stage Plan*

- *N – the difference between the Planned and Forecast Project End Dates in days, weeks or months*

- *O – the original overall effort for the project determined during project initiation and documented in the PID*

- *P – the total actual Project Effort up to the end of the previous stage*

- *Q – the total Project Effort that is now forecast as the result of preparing this Stage Plan*

- *R – the difference between Planned and Forecast Project Effort (O–Q)*

- *S – the difference between Planned and Forecast Project Effort (O–Q) expressed as a percentage of the Planned Project Effort*

- *T – the original overall cost for the project determined during project initiation and documented in the PID*

- *U – the total actual Project Cost up to the end of the previous stage*

- *V – the total Project Cost that is now forecast as the result of preparing this Stage Plan*

- *W – the difference between Planned and Forecast Project Cost (T–V)*

- *X – the difference between Planned and Forecast Project Cost (T–V) expressed as a percentage of the Planned Project Cost*

BUSINESS CASE IMPACT

Identify any changes to the expected benefits resulting from the Stage Plan or confirm that the Business Case expectations have not changed.

STAGE PLAN

Stage Product Breakdown Structure – see Appendix 1
Stage Product Descriptions – see Appendix 2
Stage Product Flow Diagram – see Appendix 3
Stage Gantt Chart – see Appendix 4
Table of Resource Requirements for Stage – see Appendix 5

INDEX